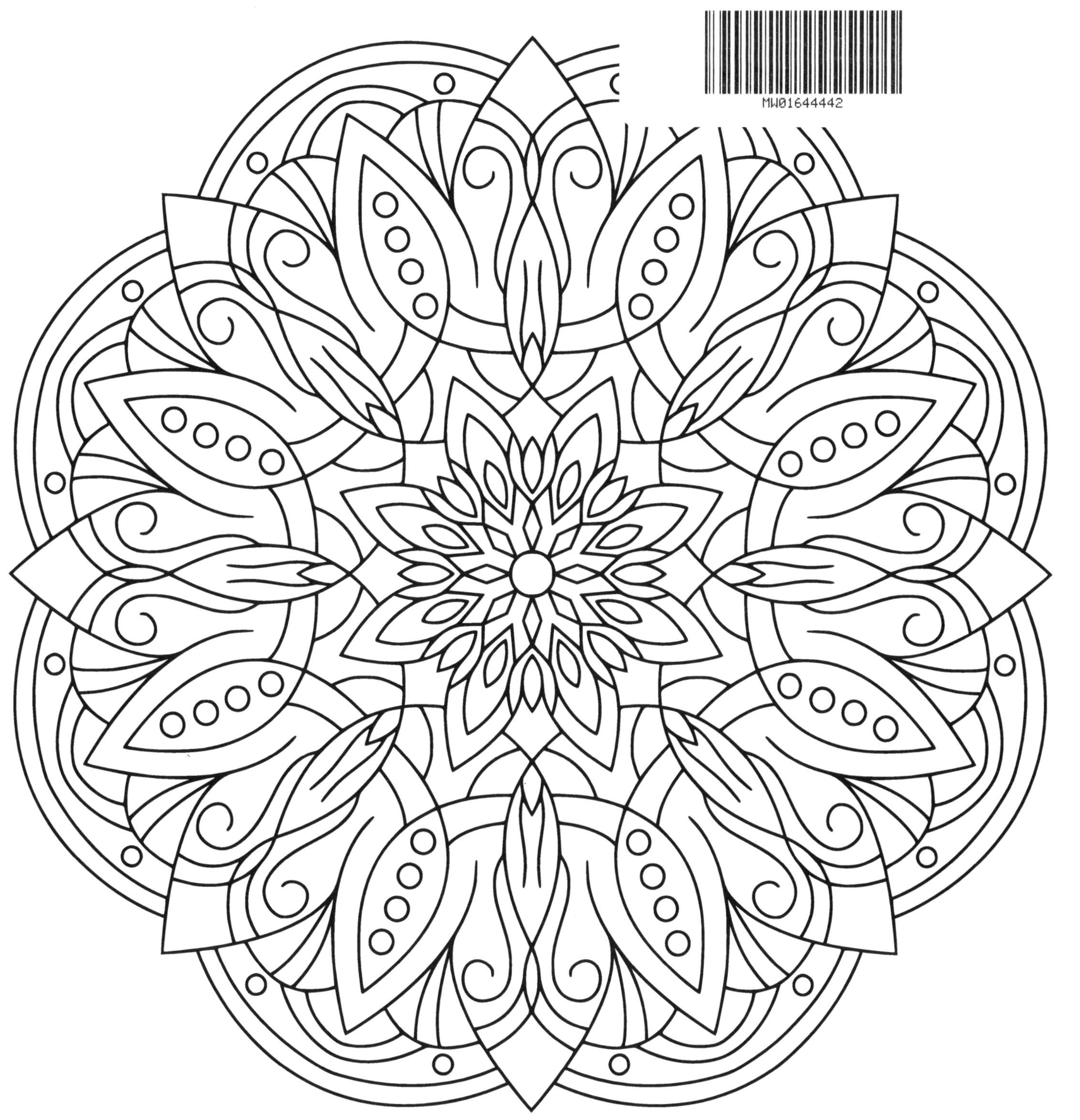
MW01644442

Zendipity Mandala Mindfulness and Relaxation Adult COLORING Book:

Bold, Easy-to-Color Patterns For Anxiety and Stress Relief

Color Your World Calm

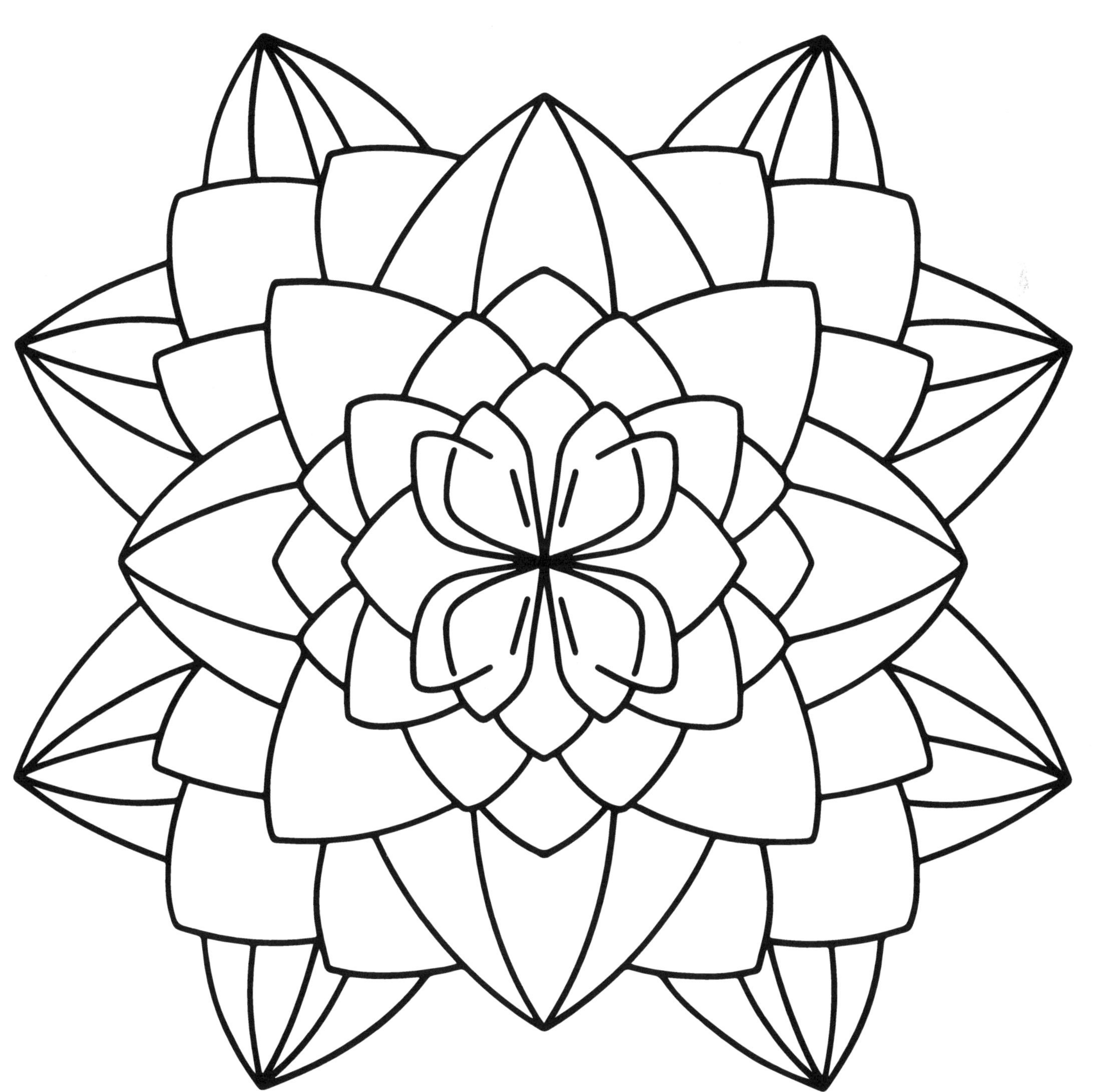

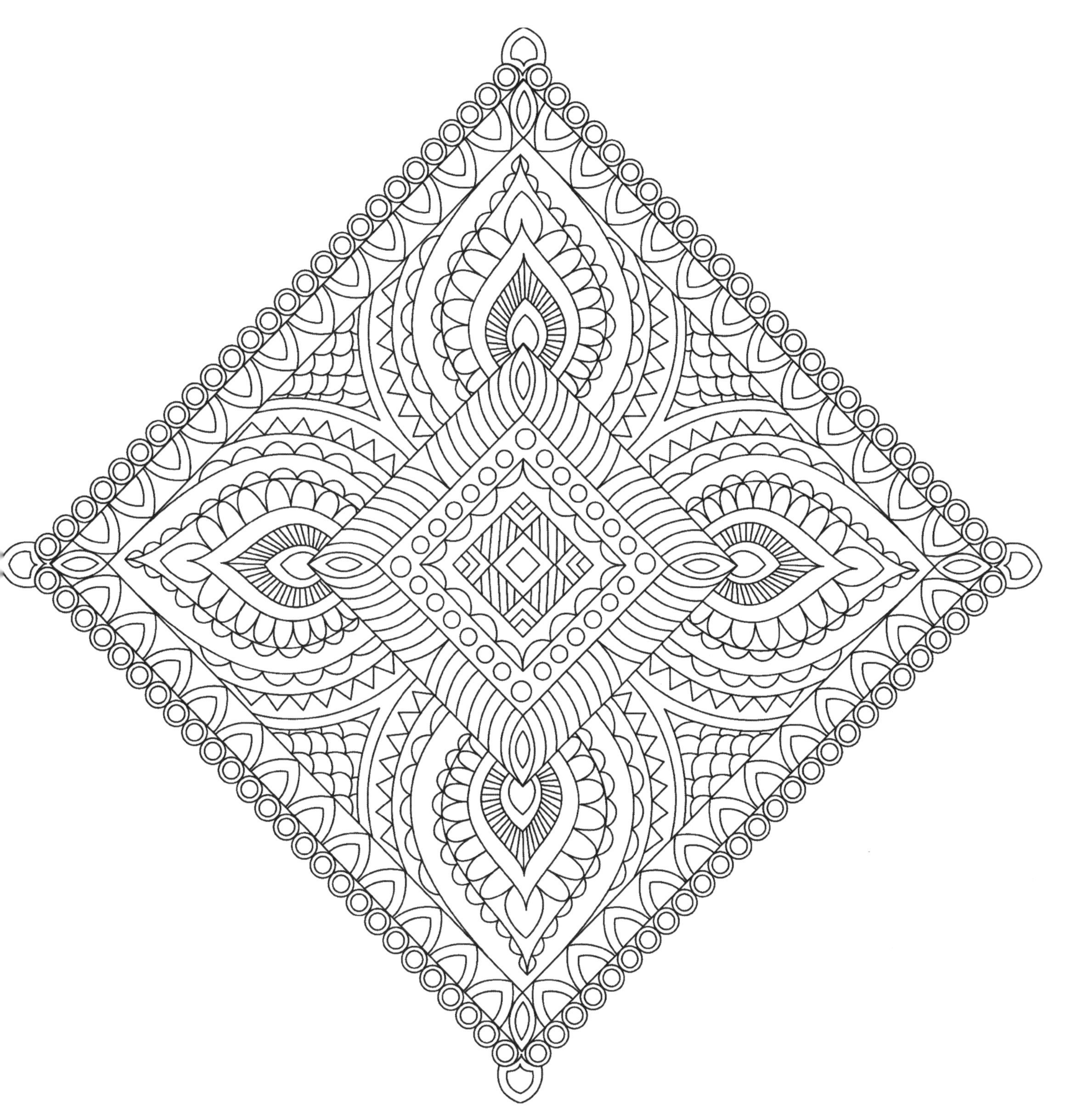

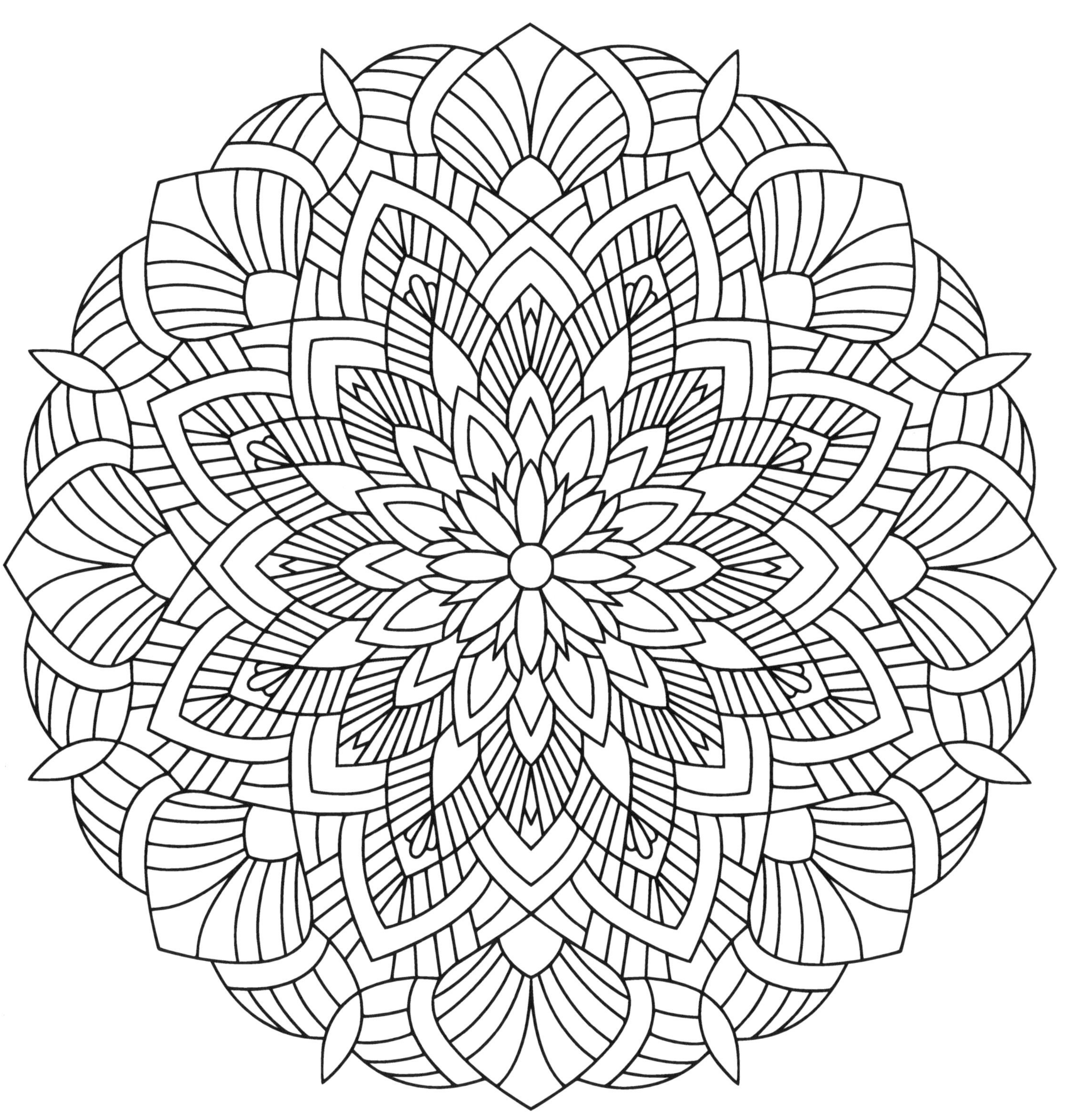

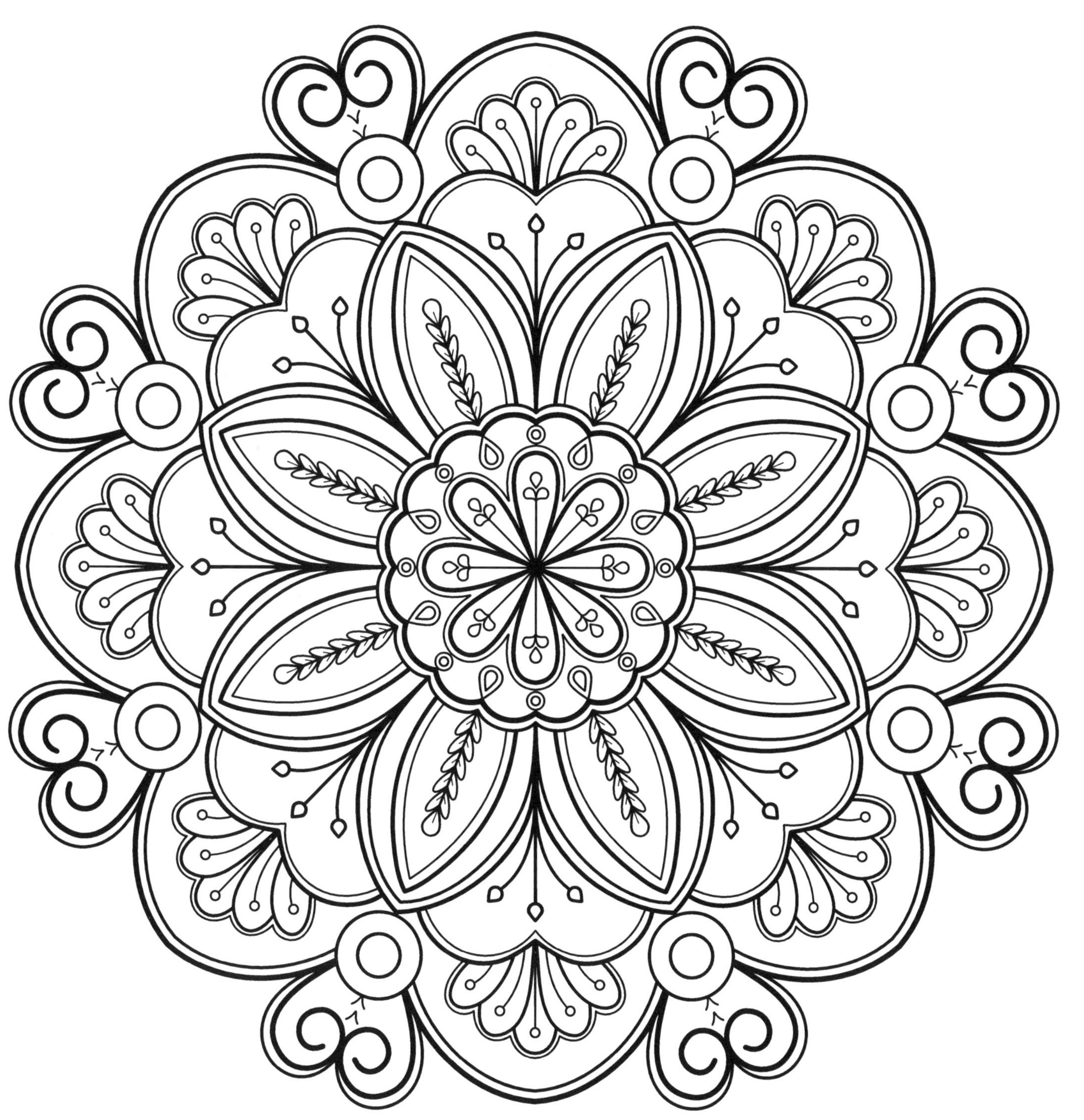

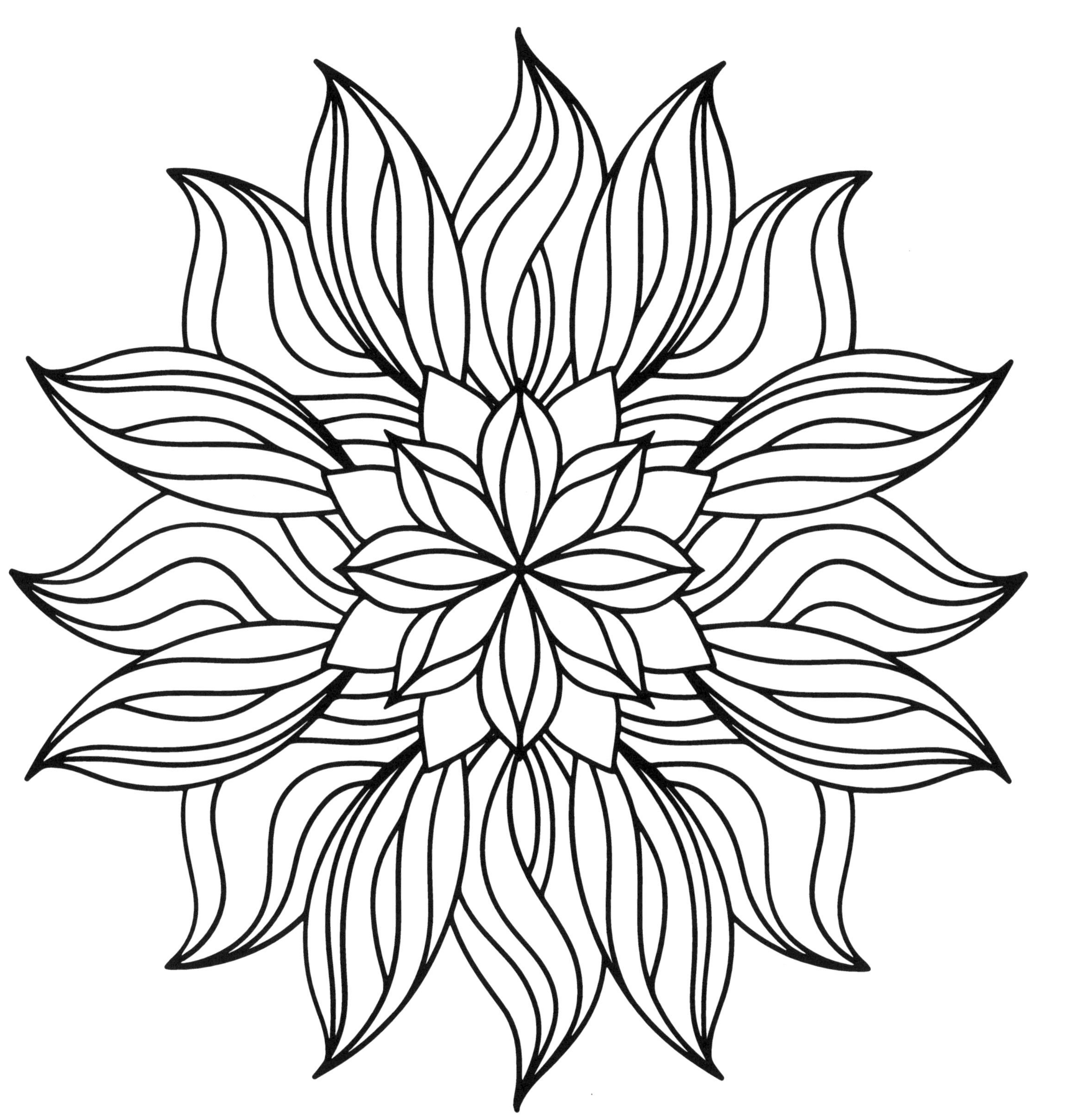

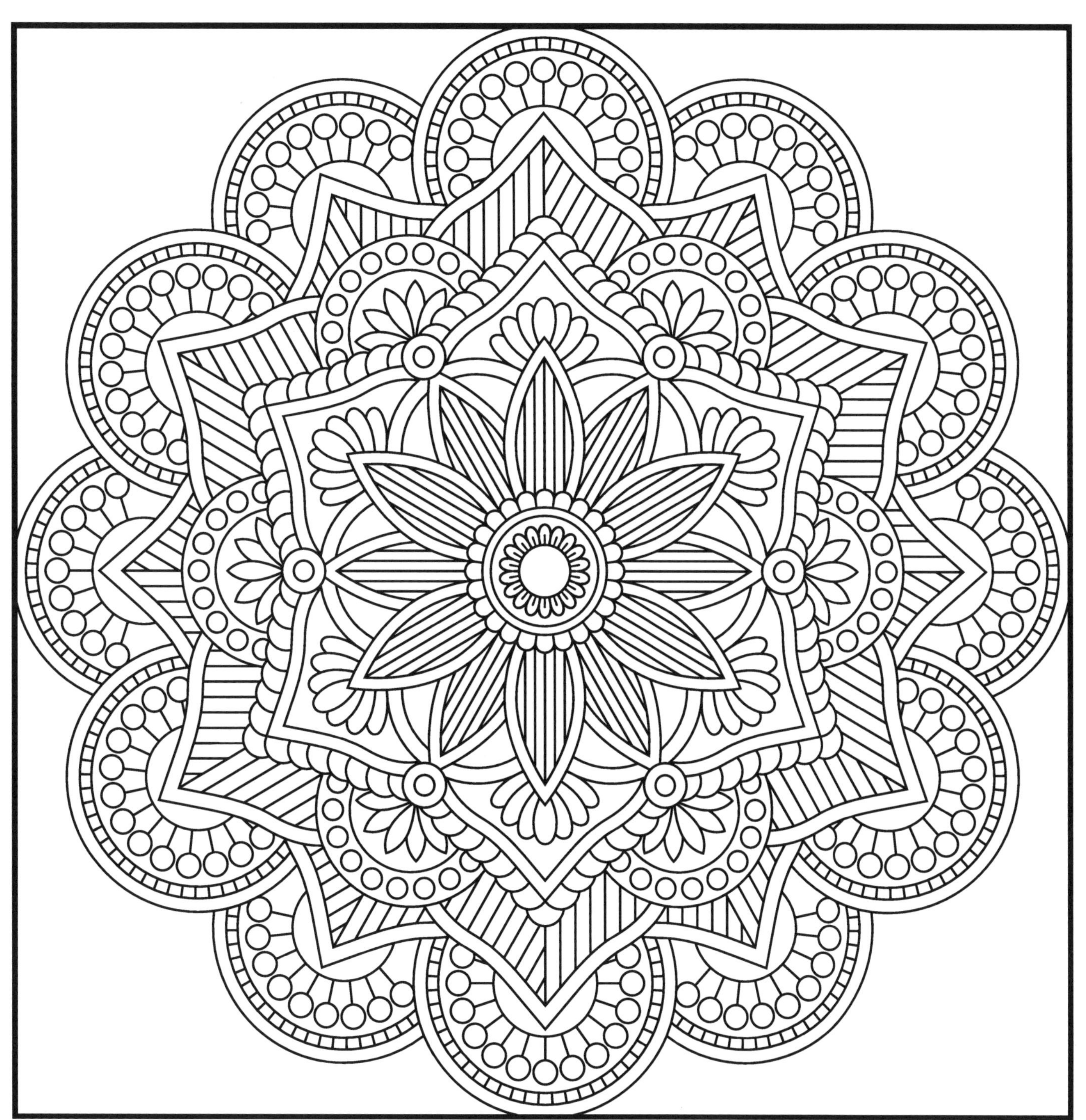

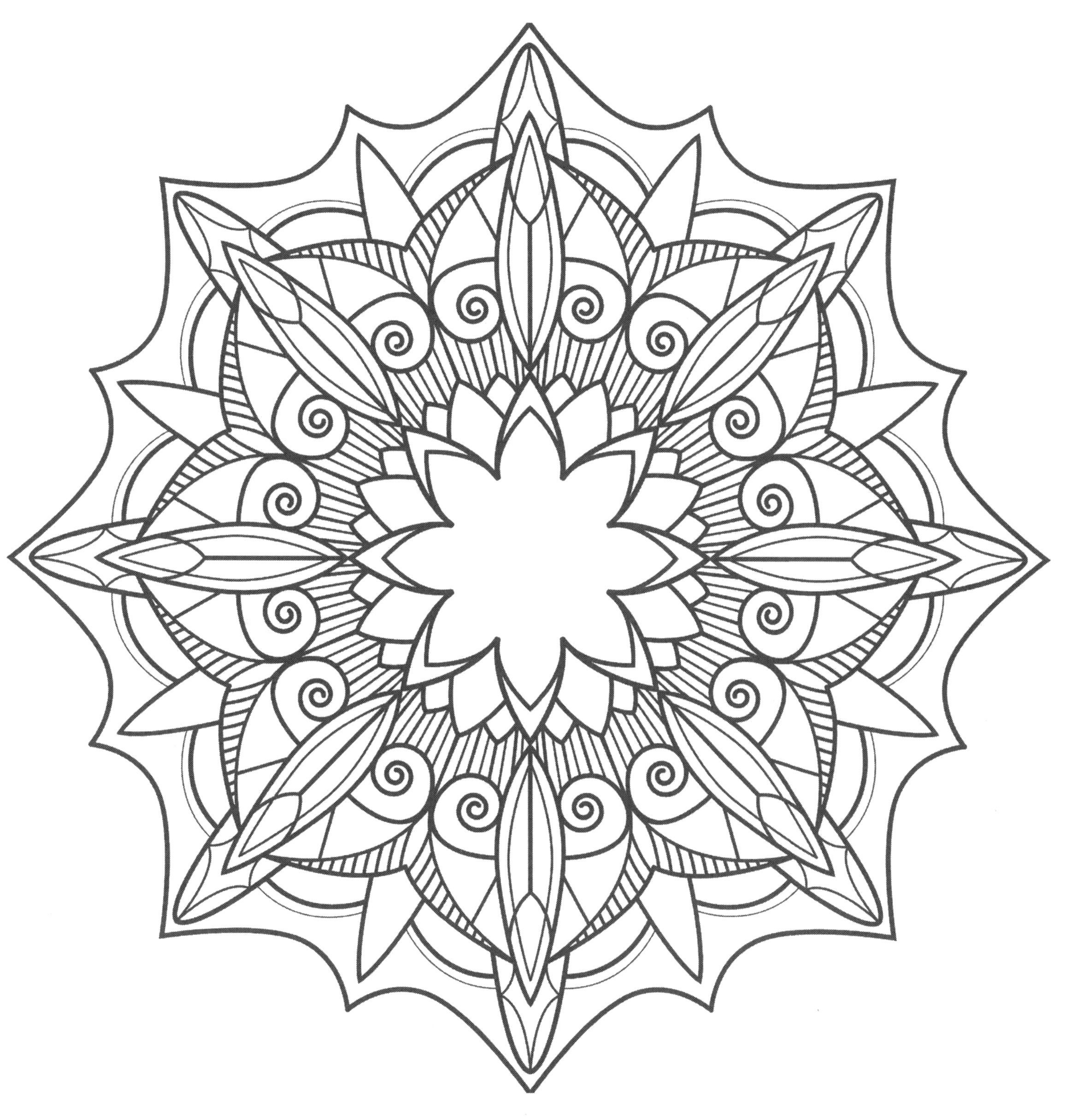

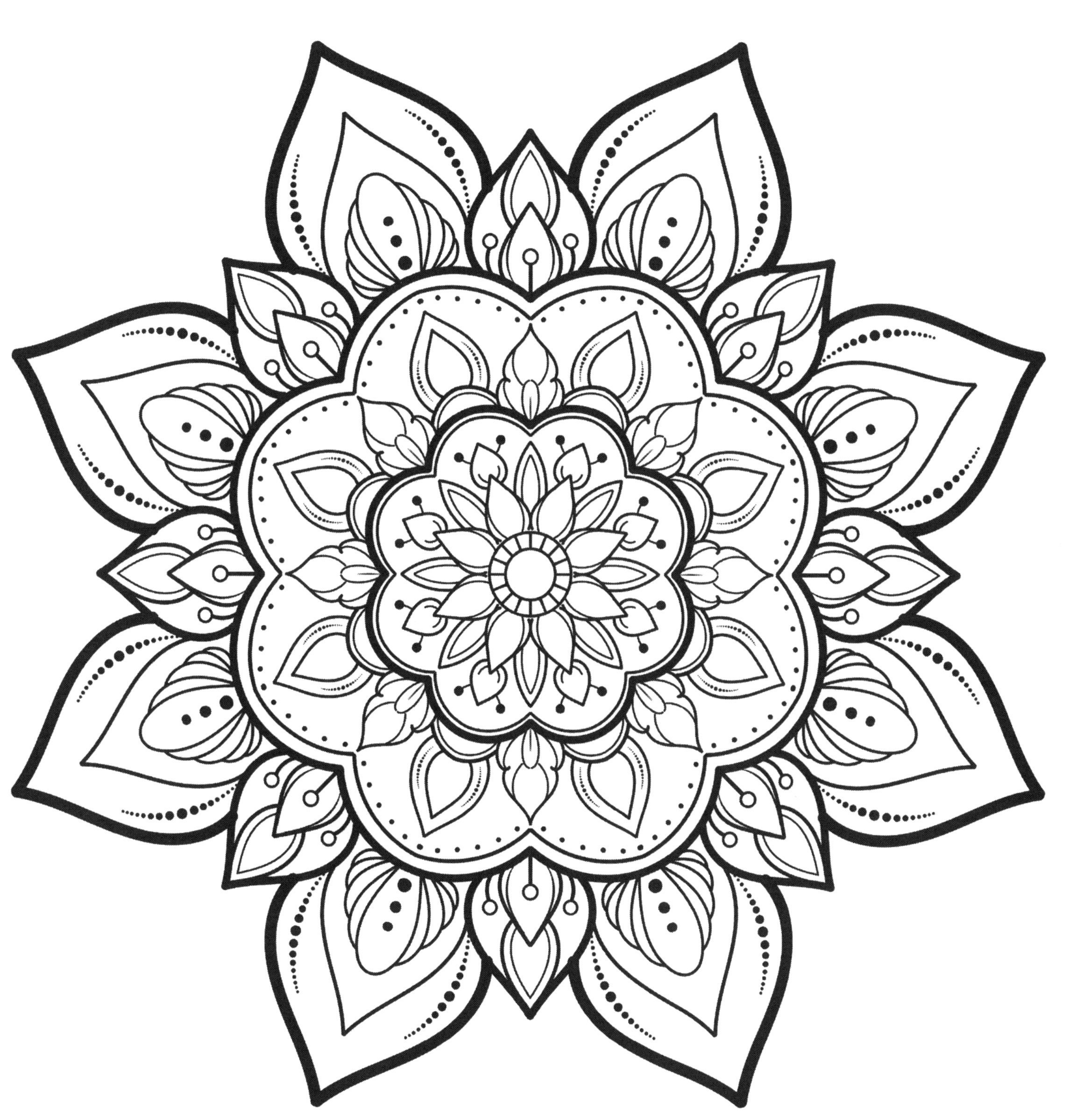

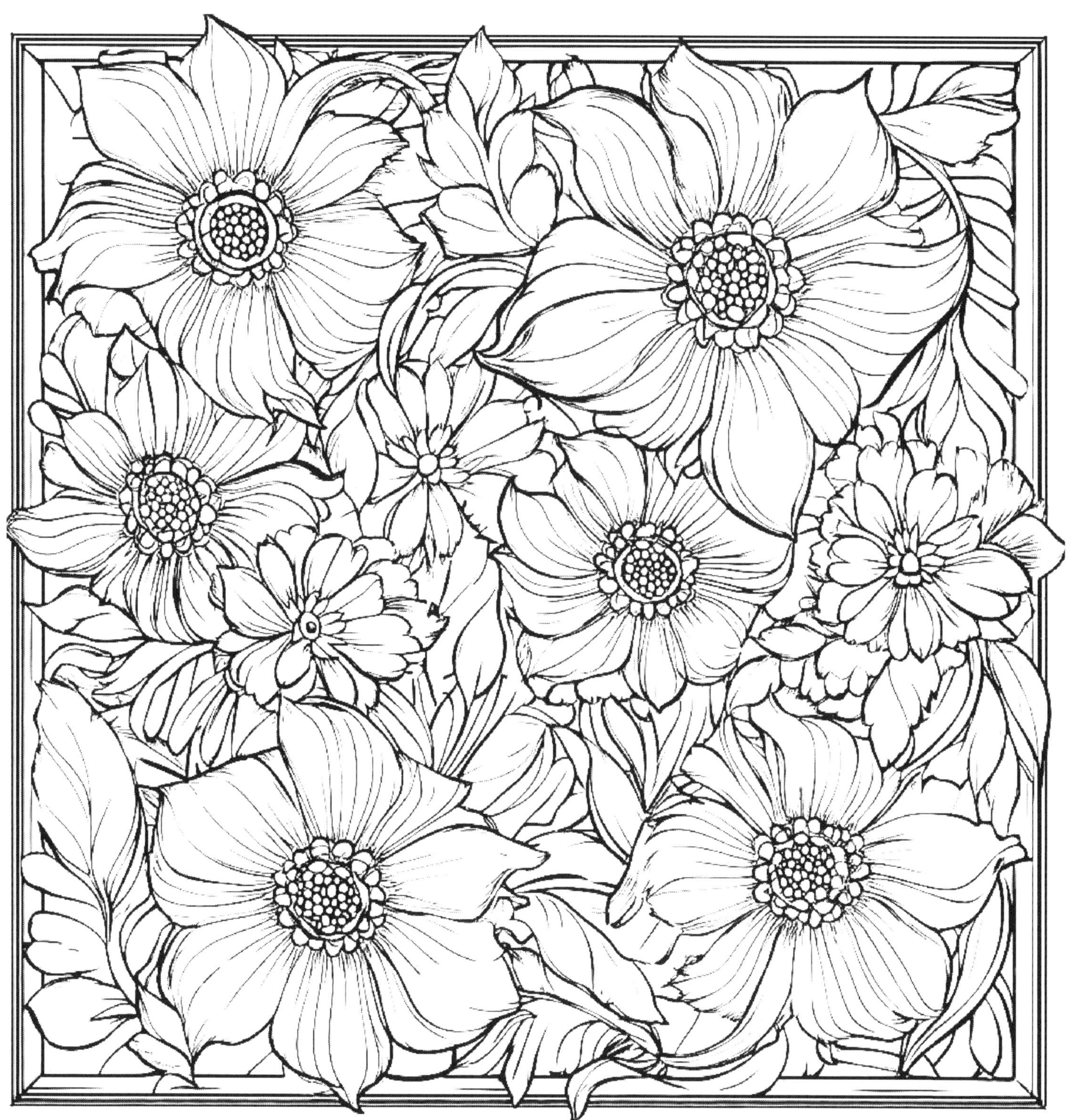

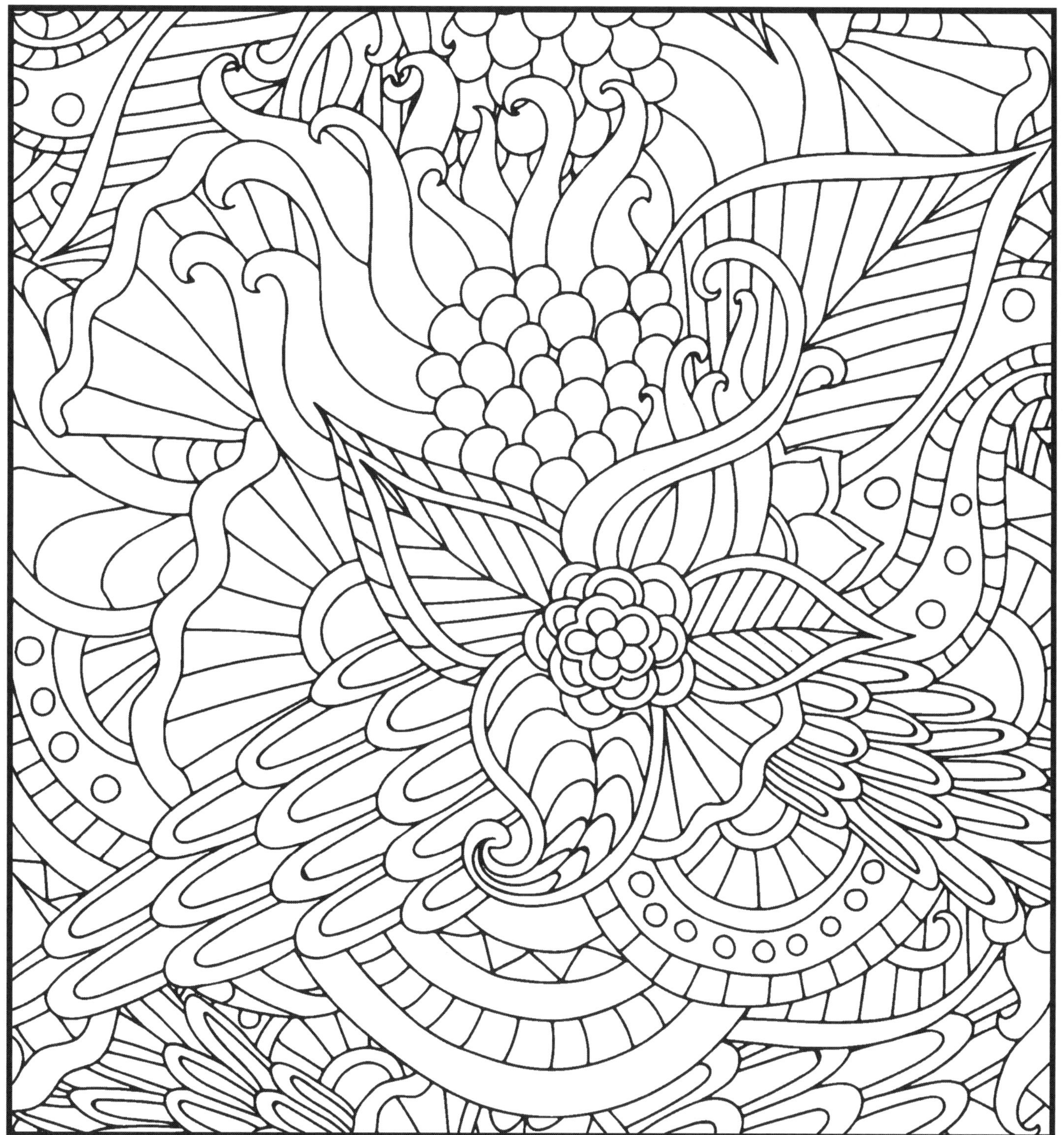

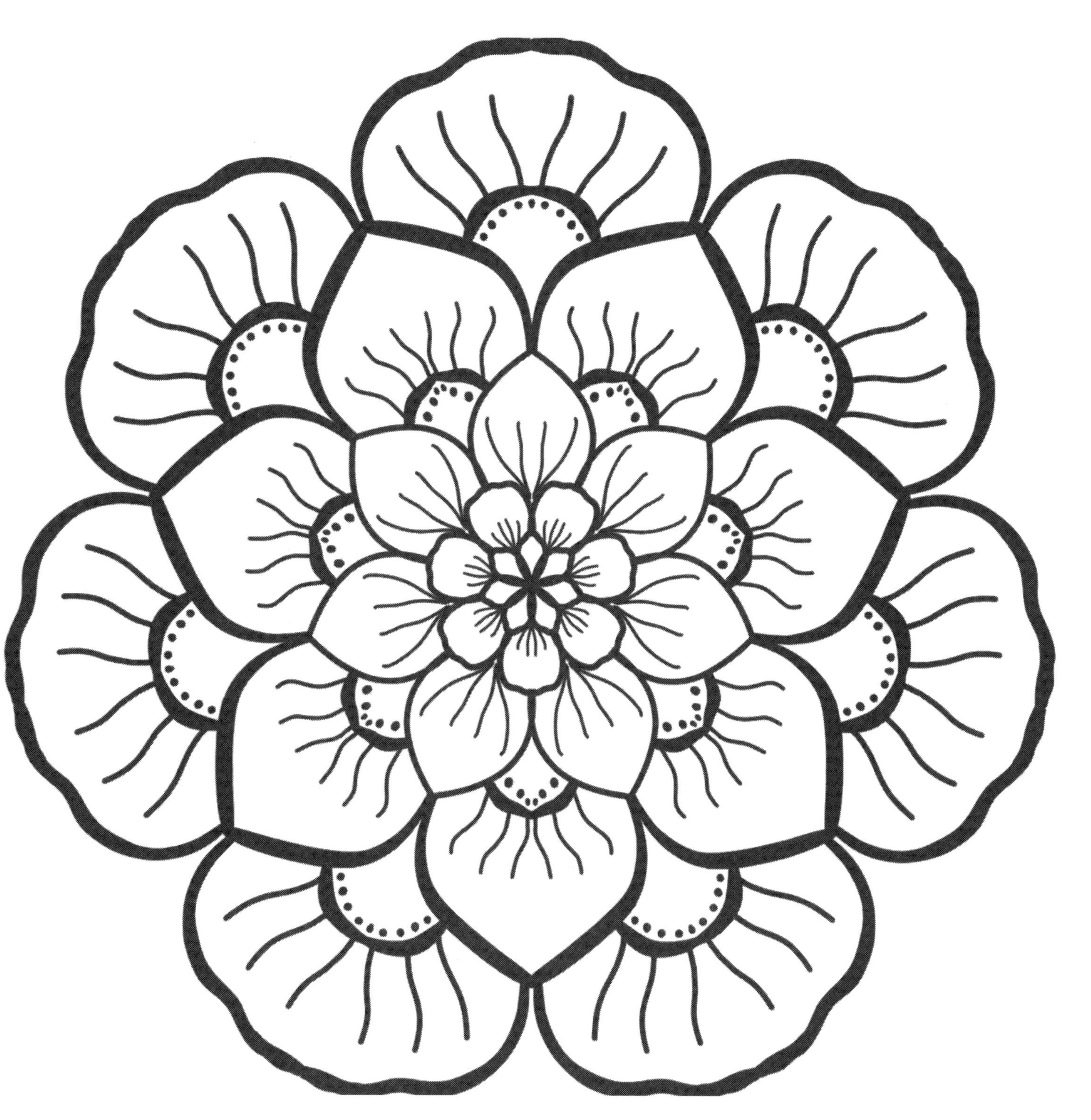

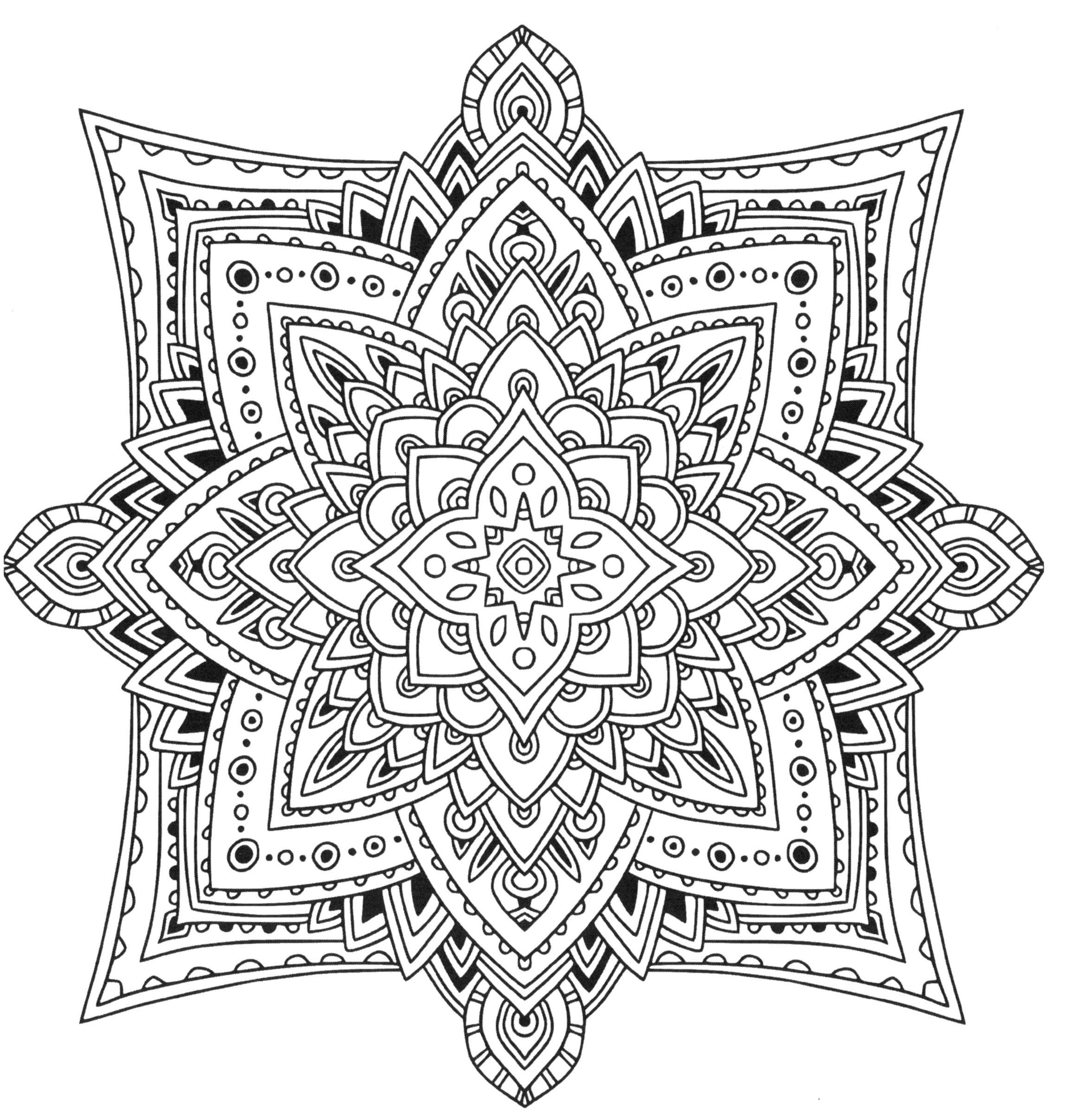

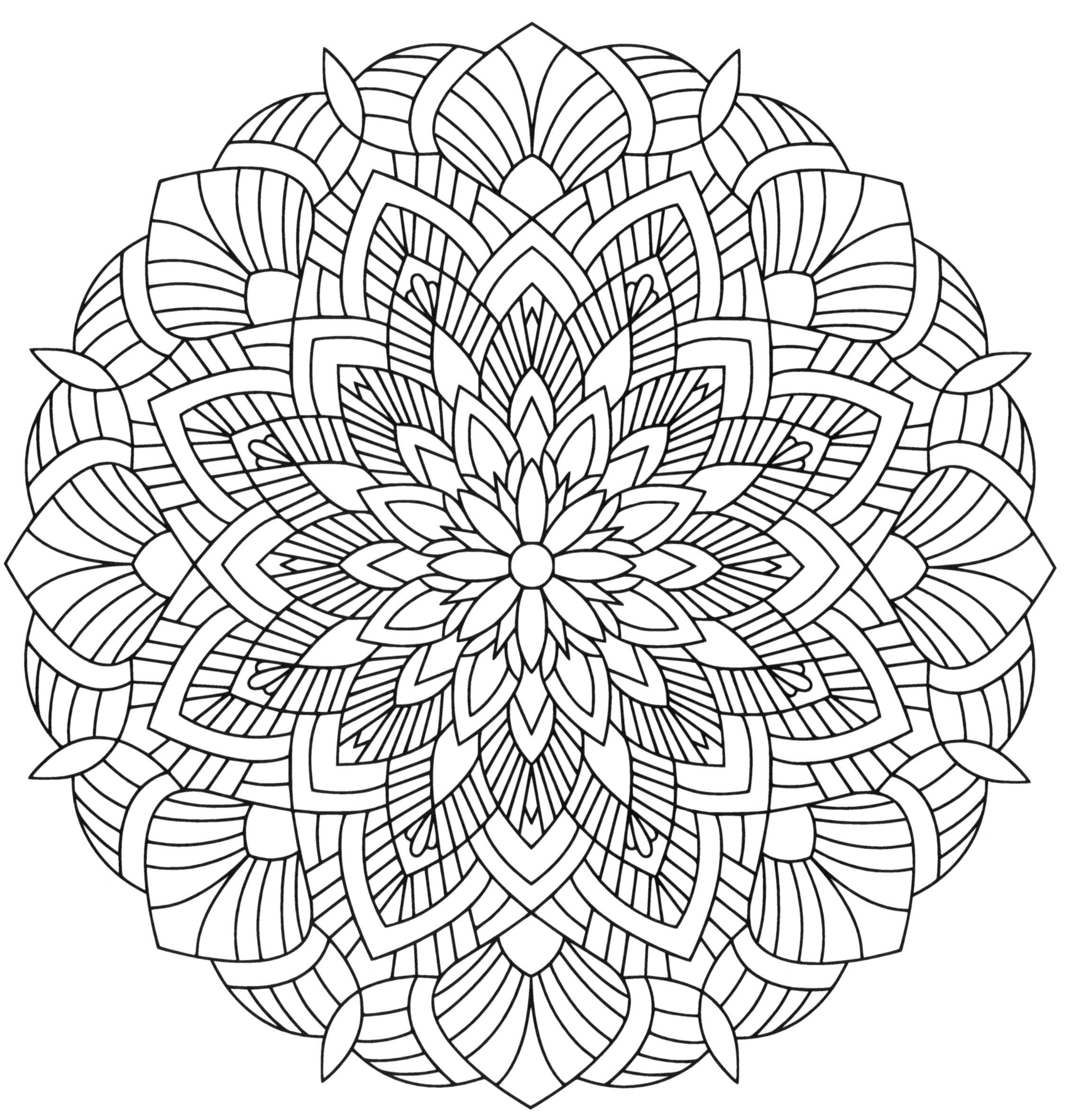

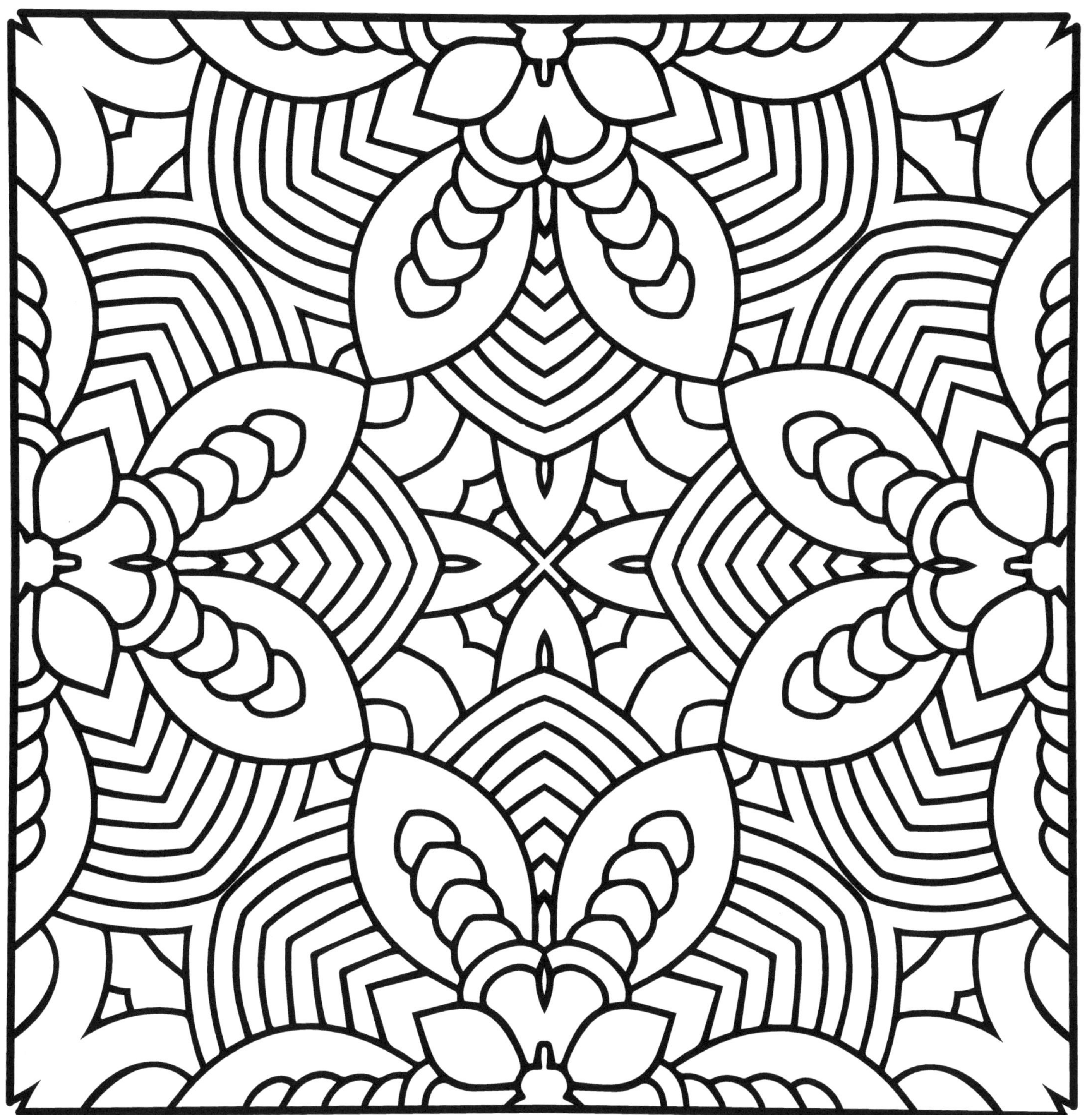

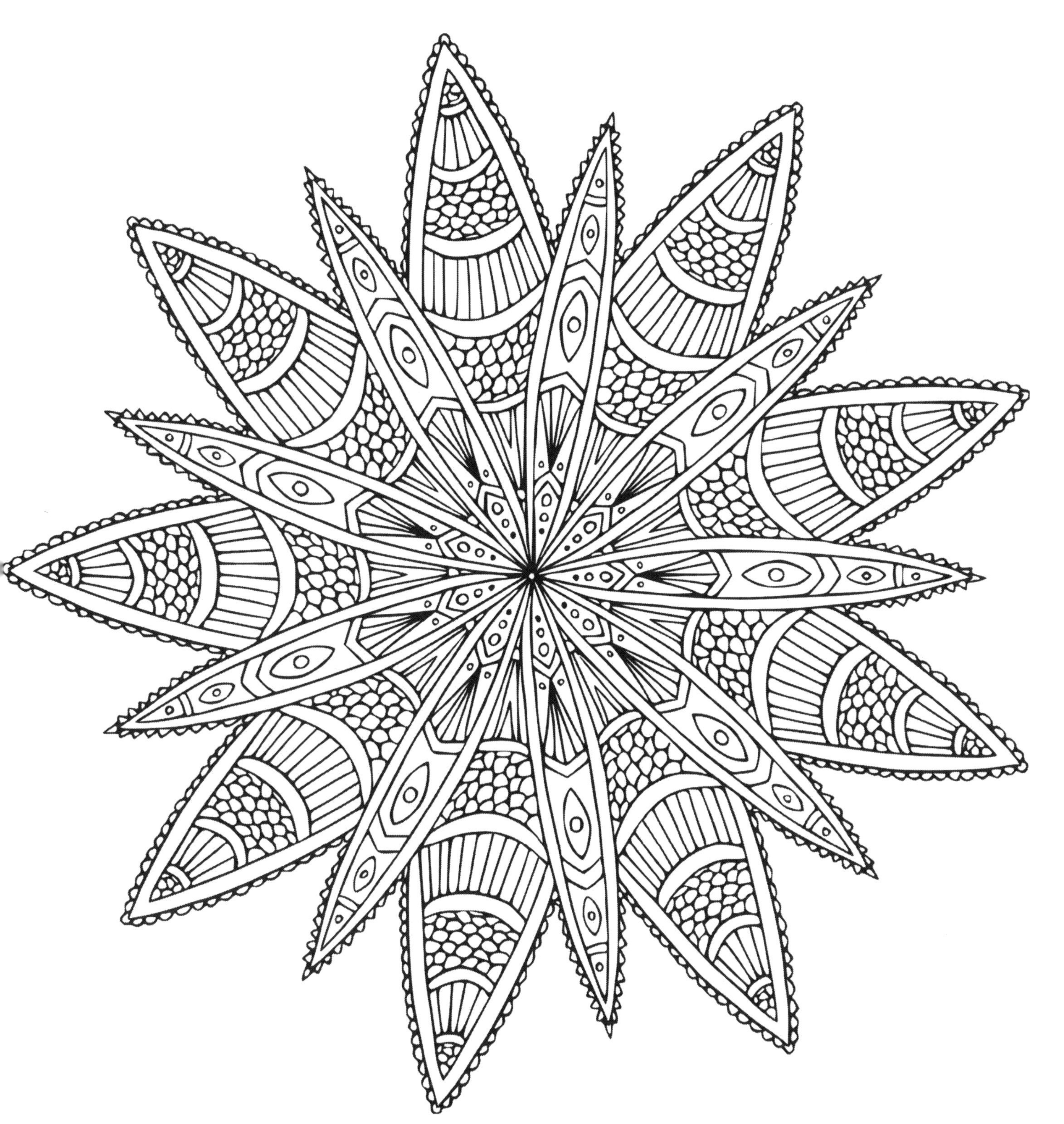

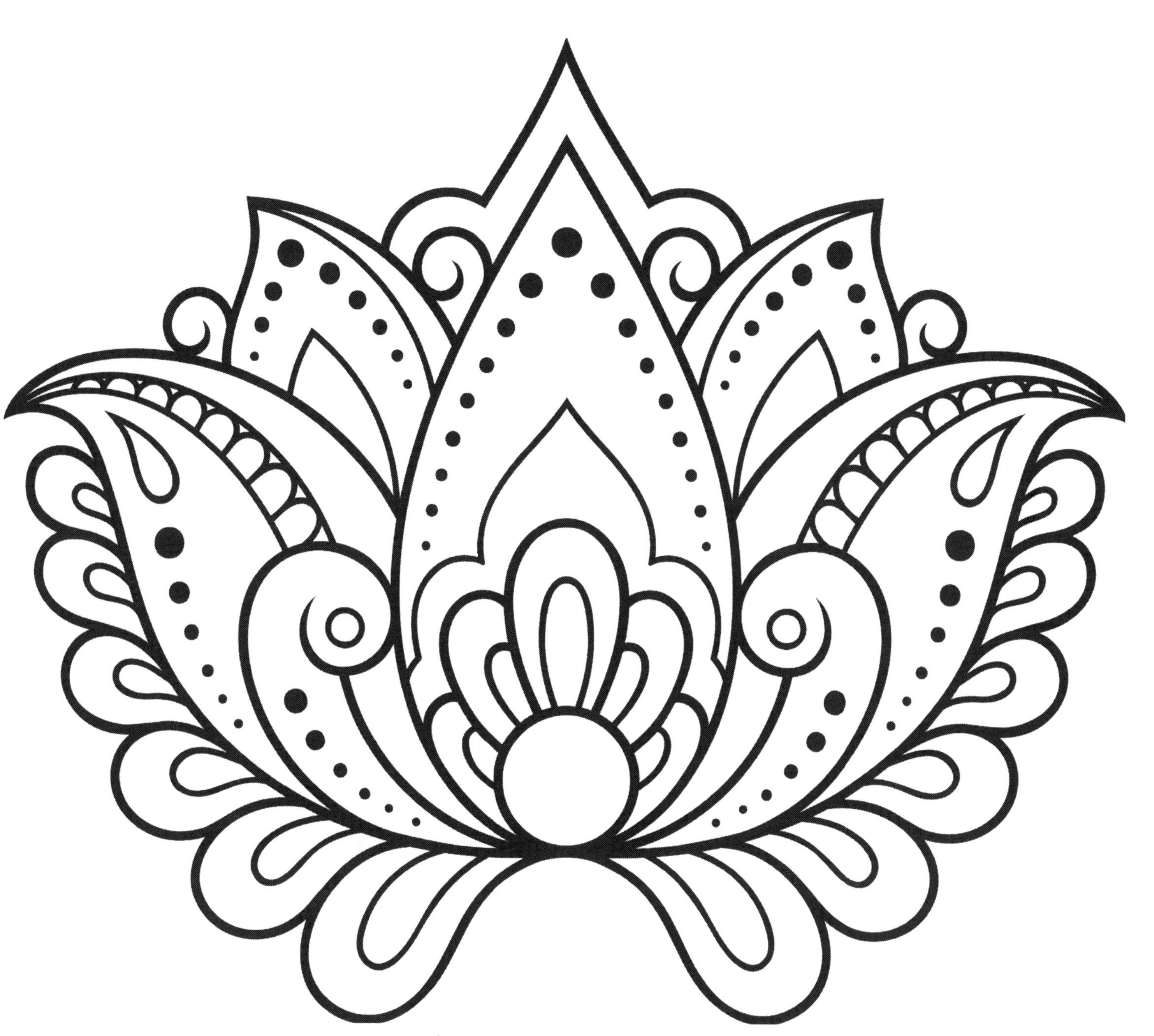

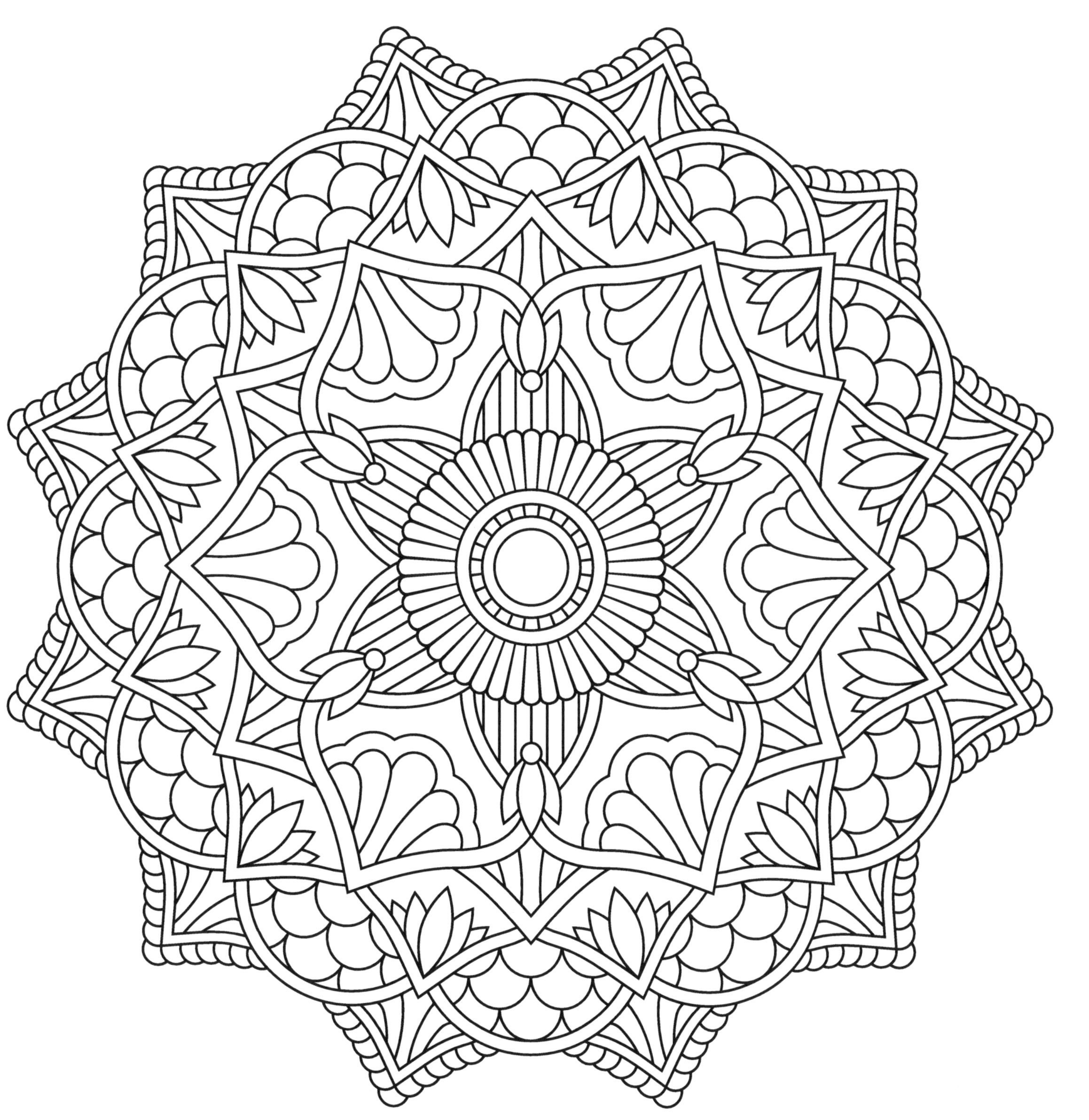

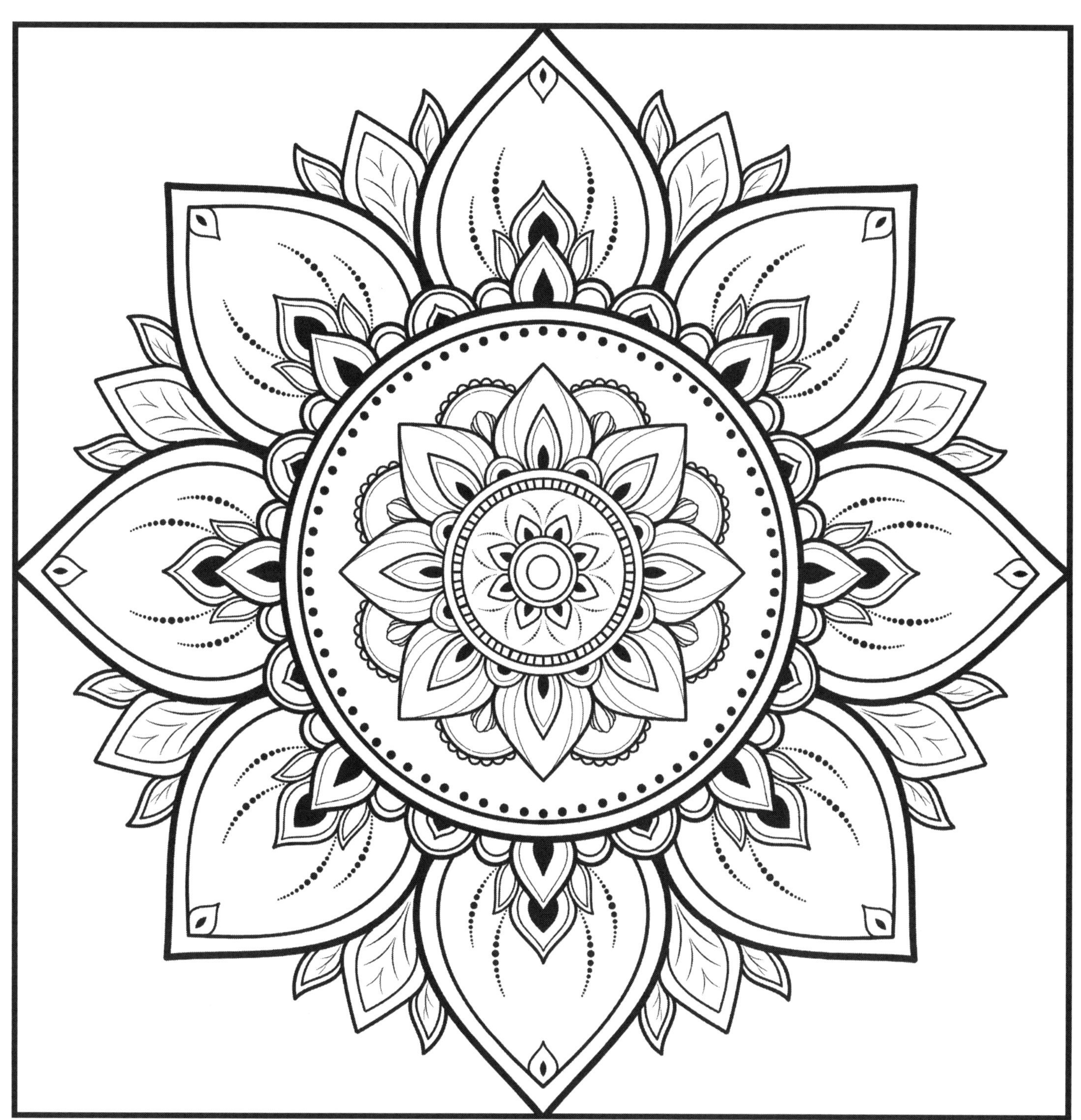

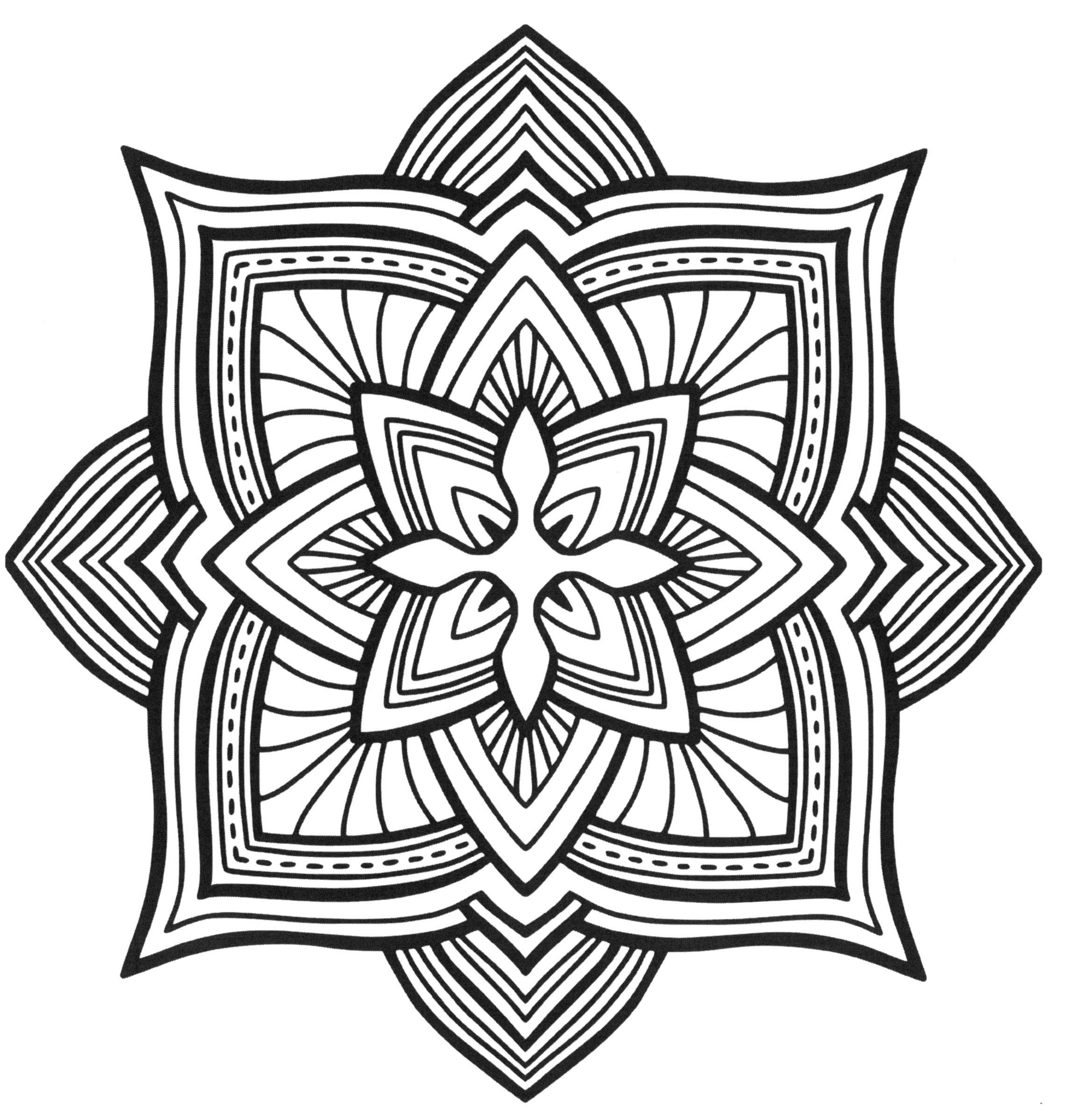

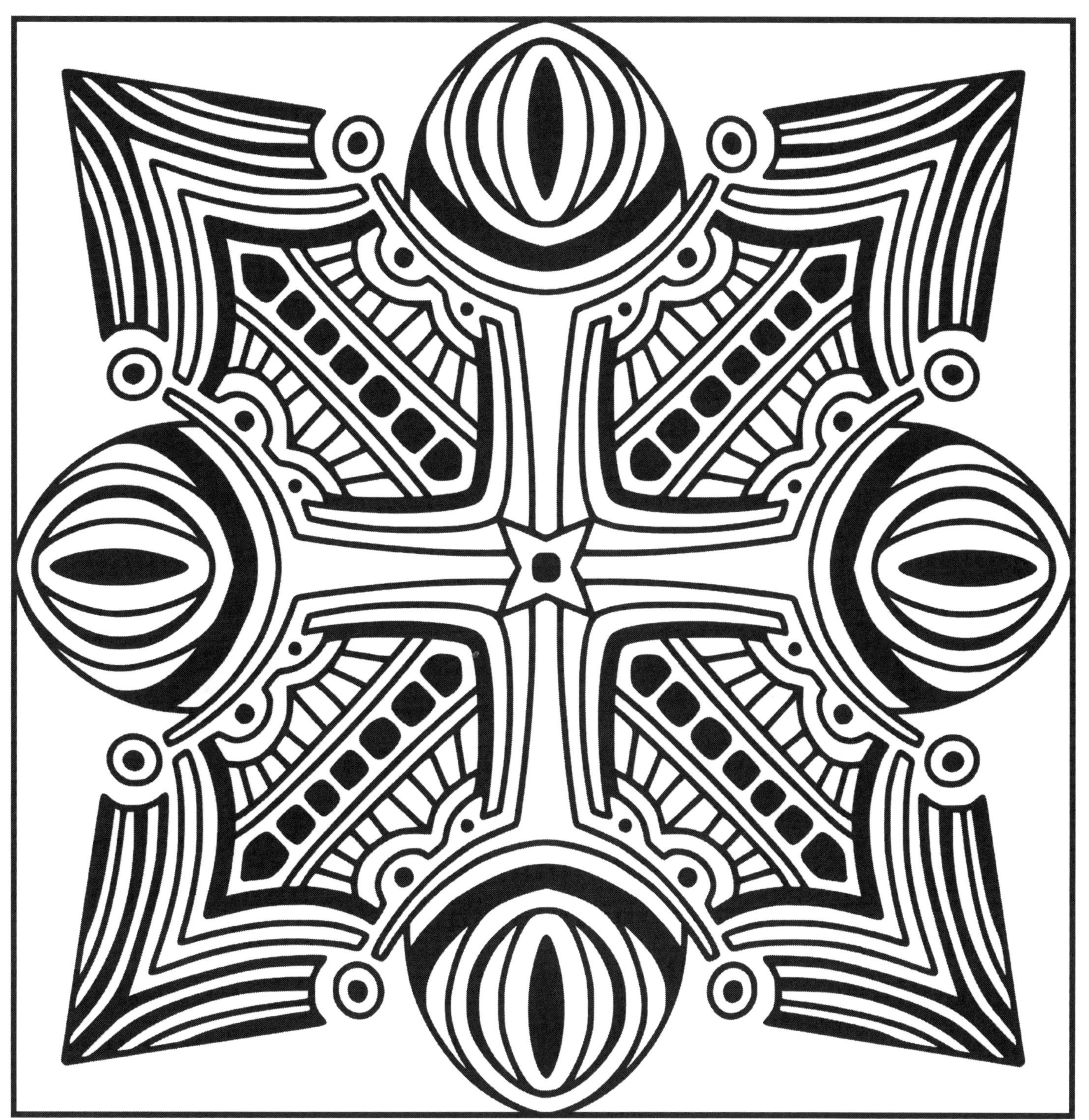

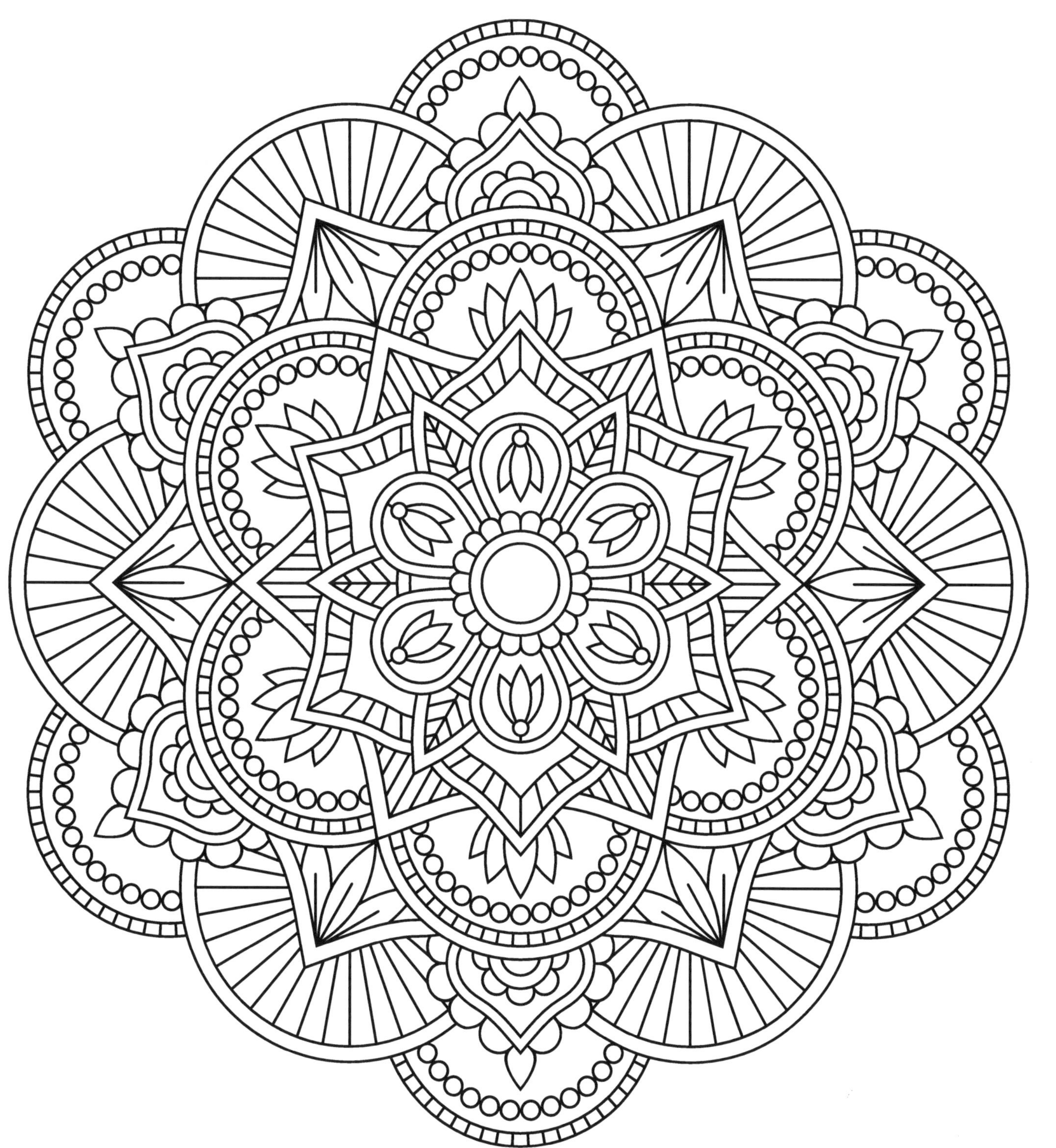

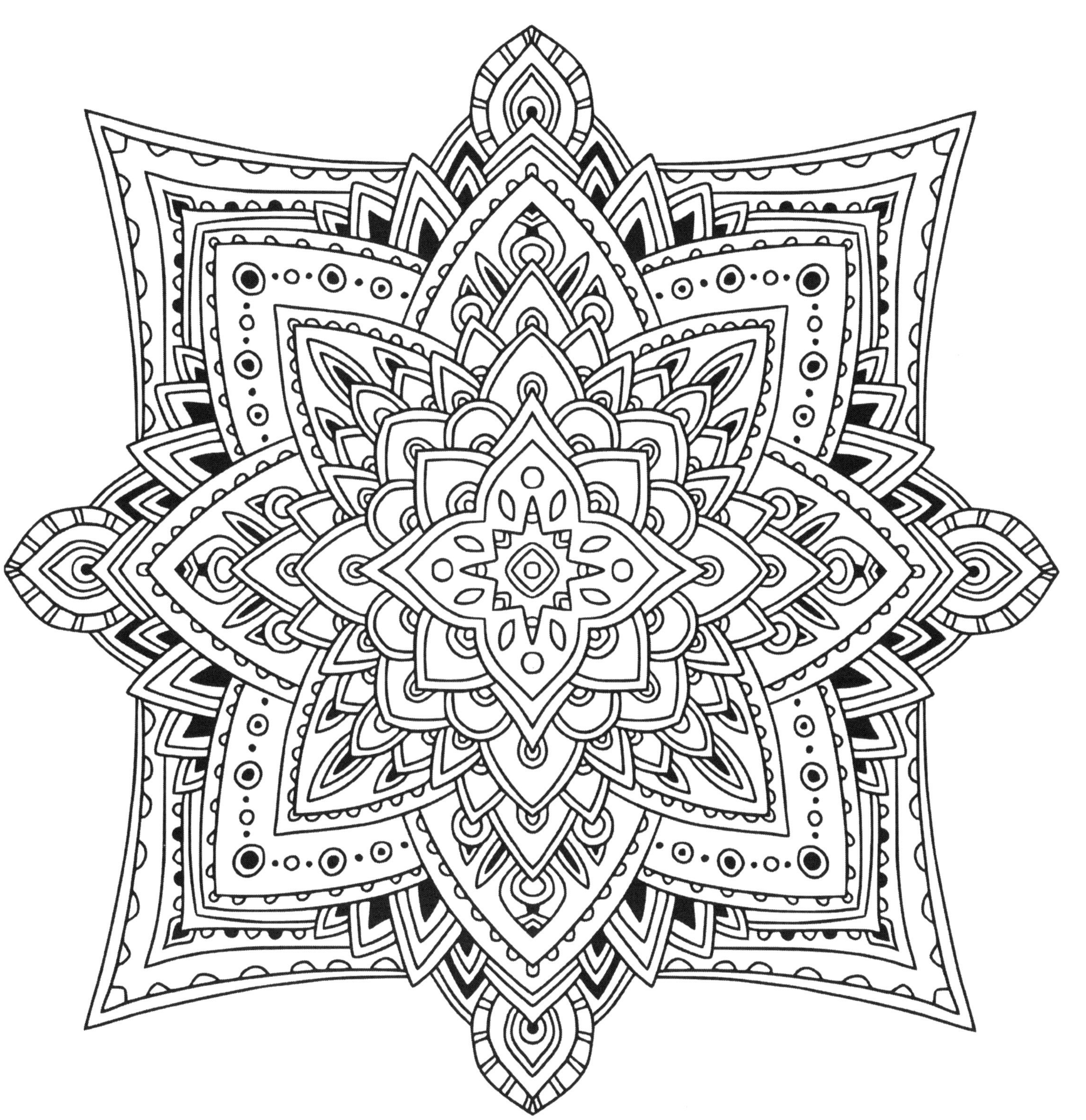

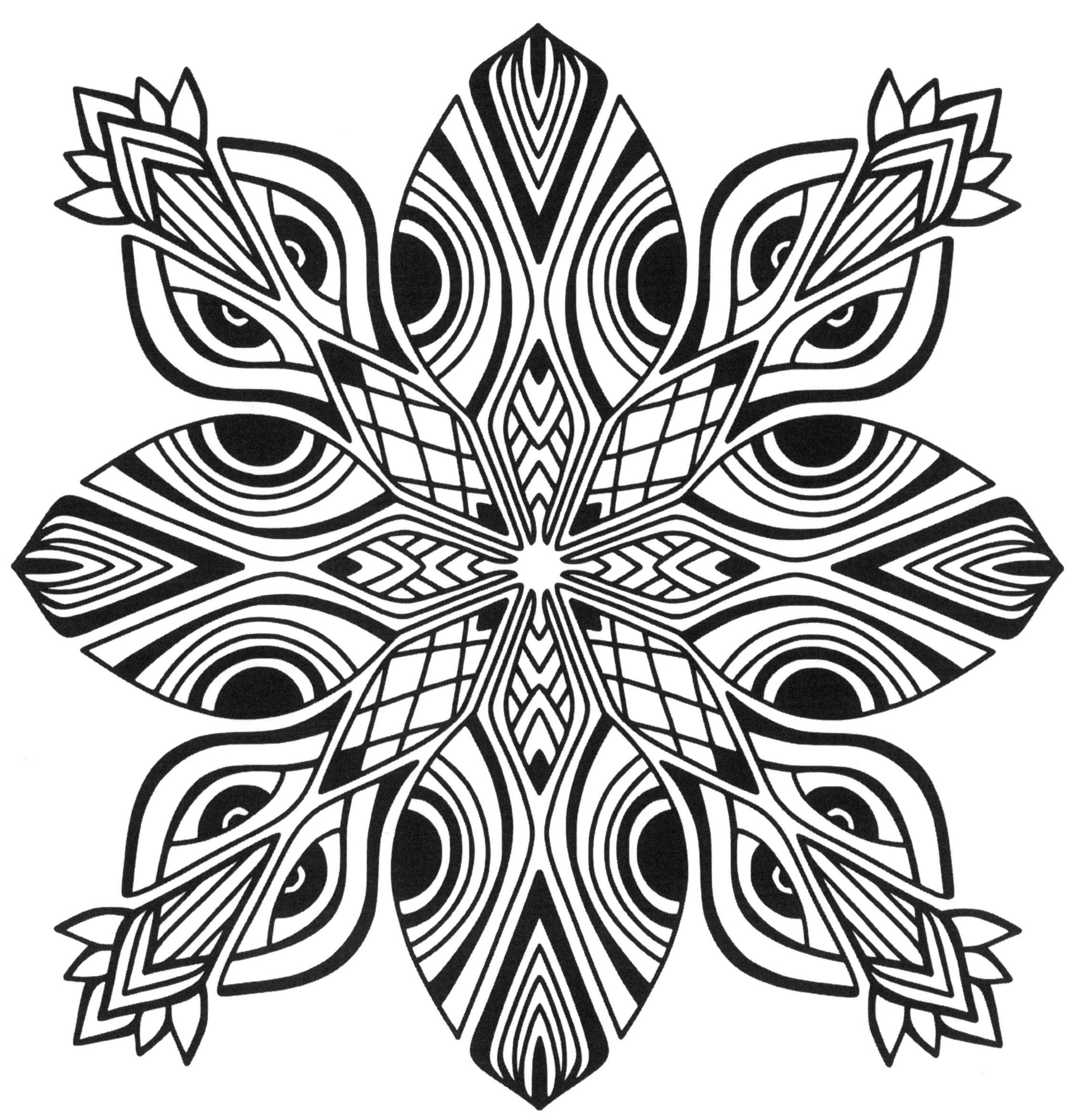

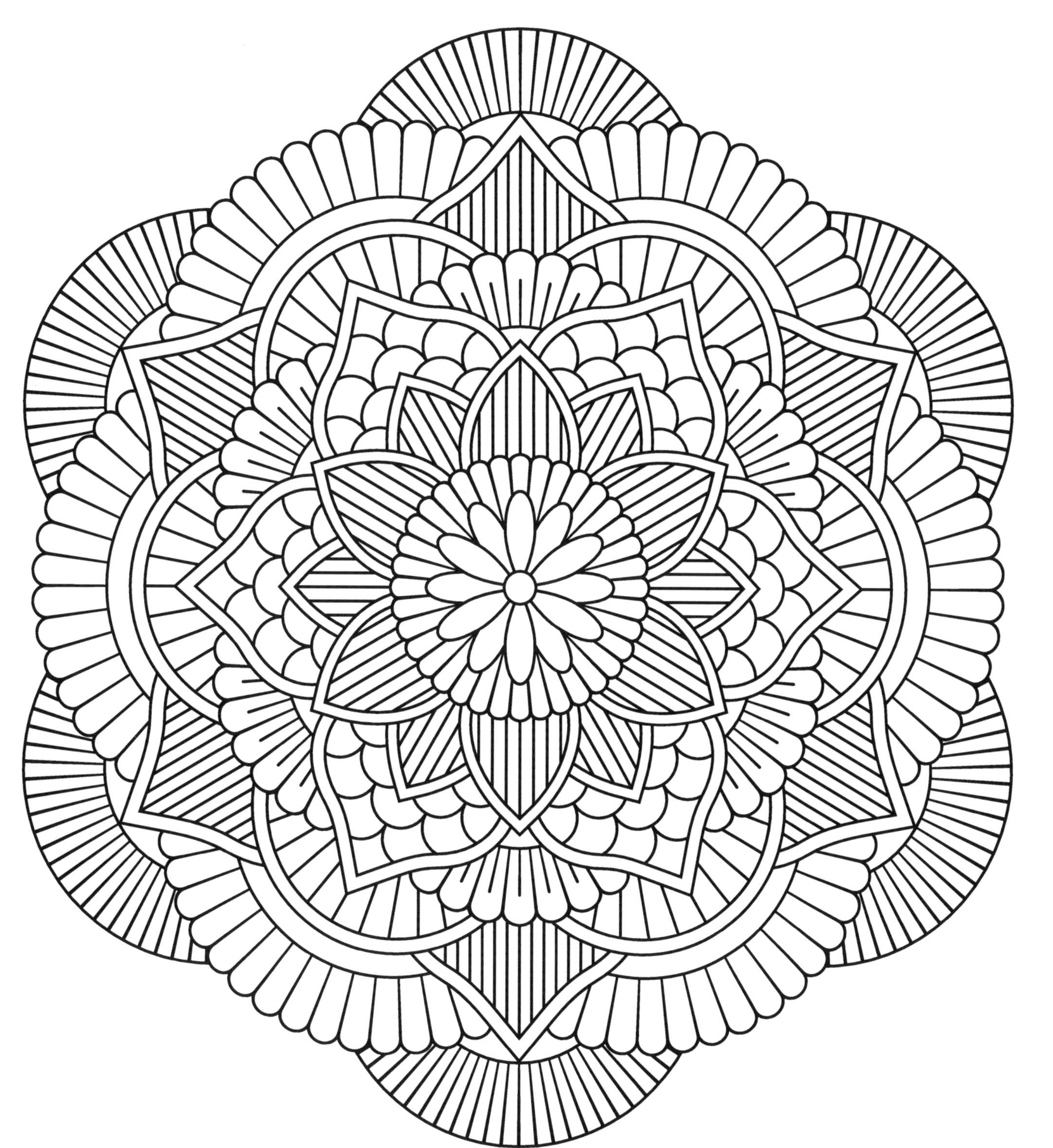

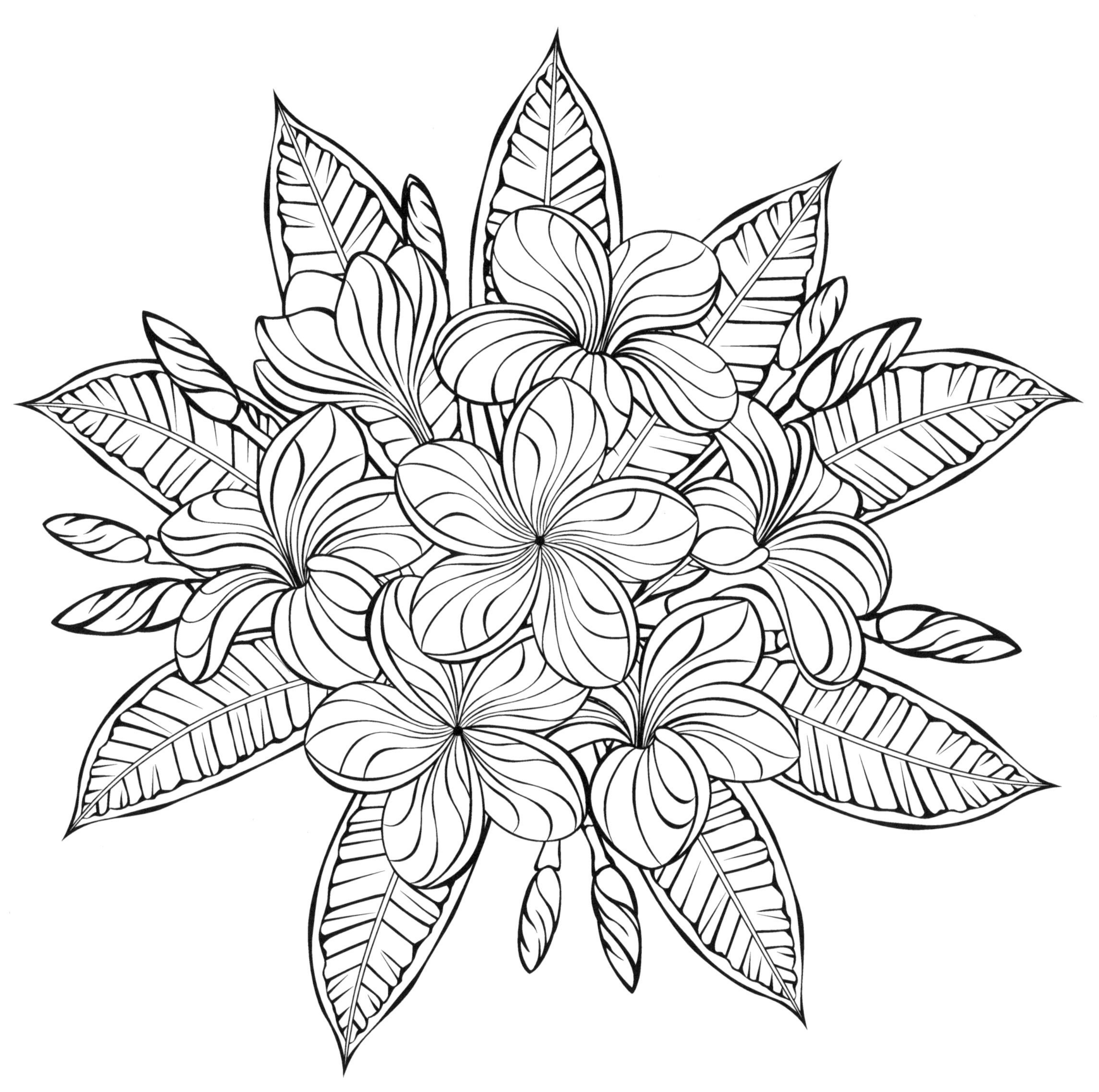

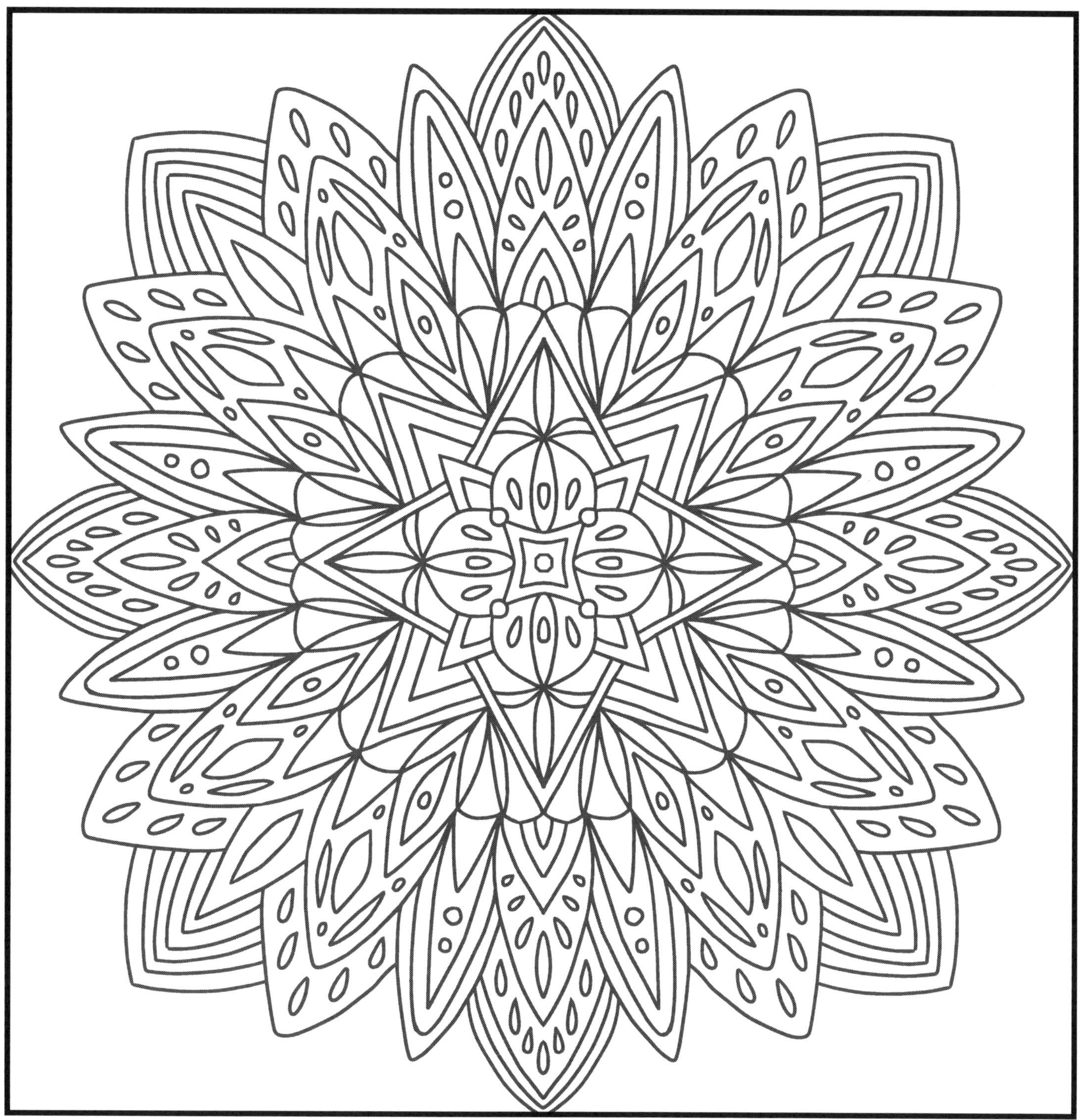

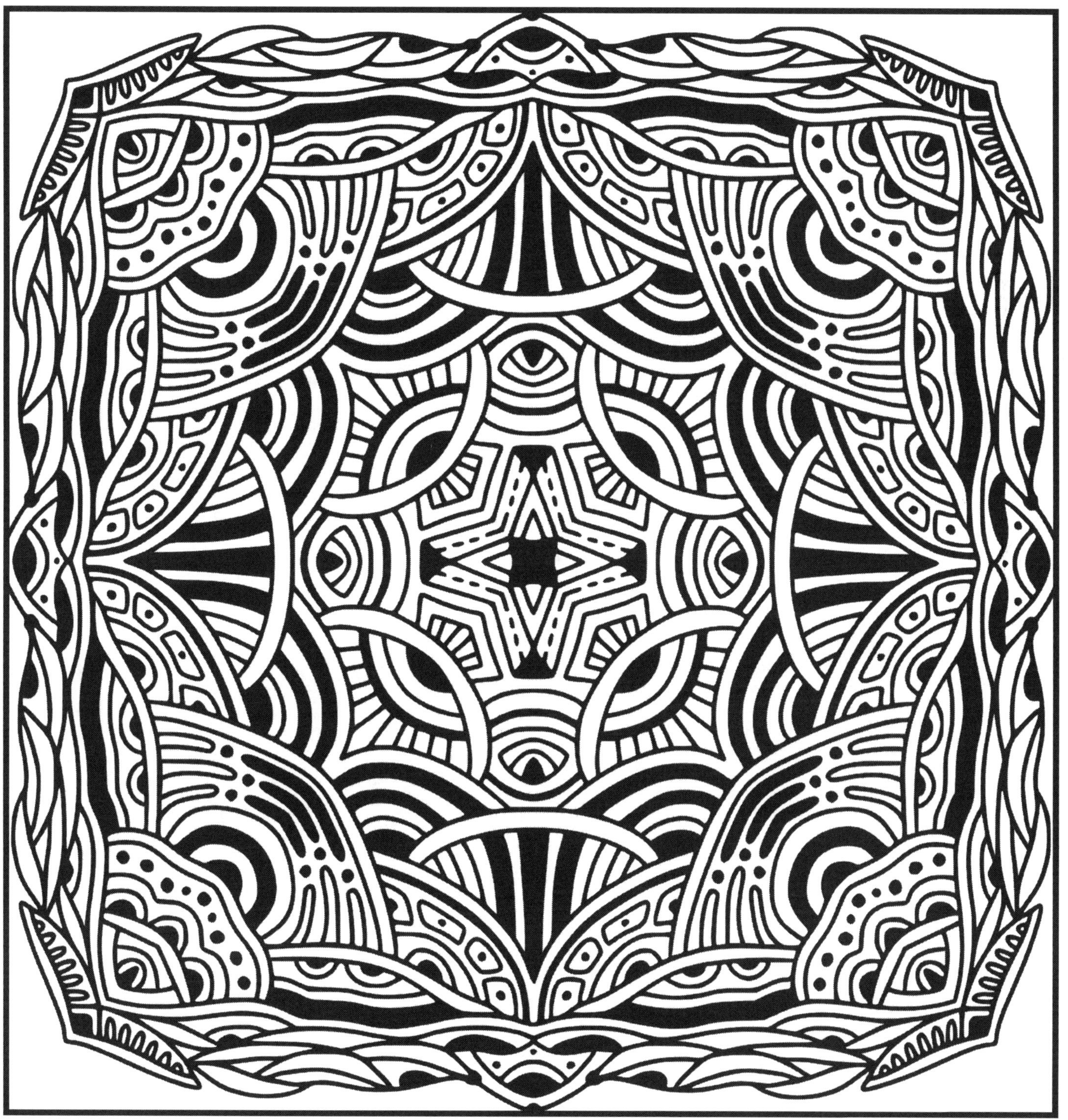

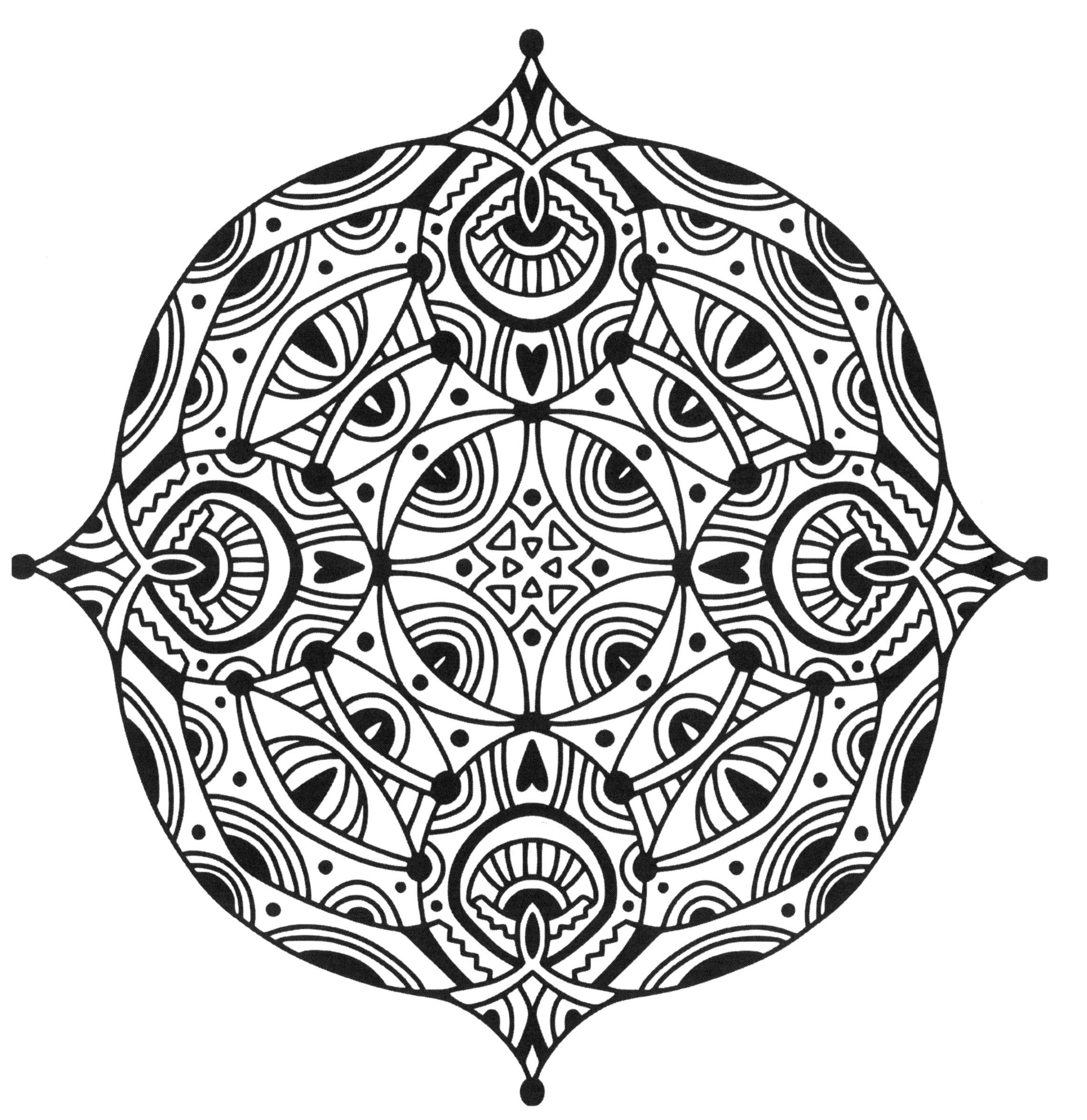

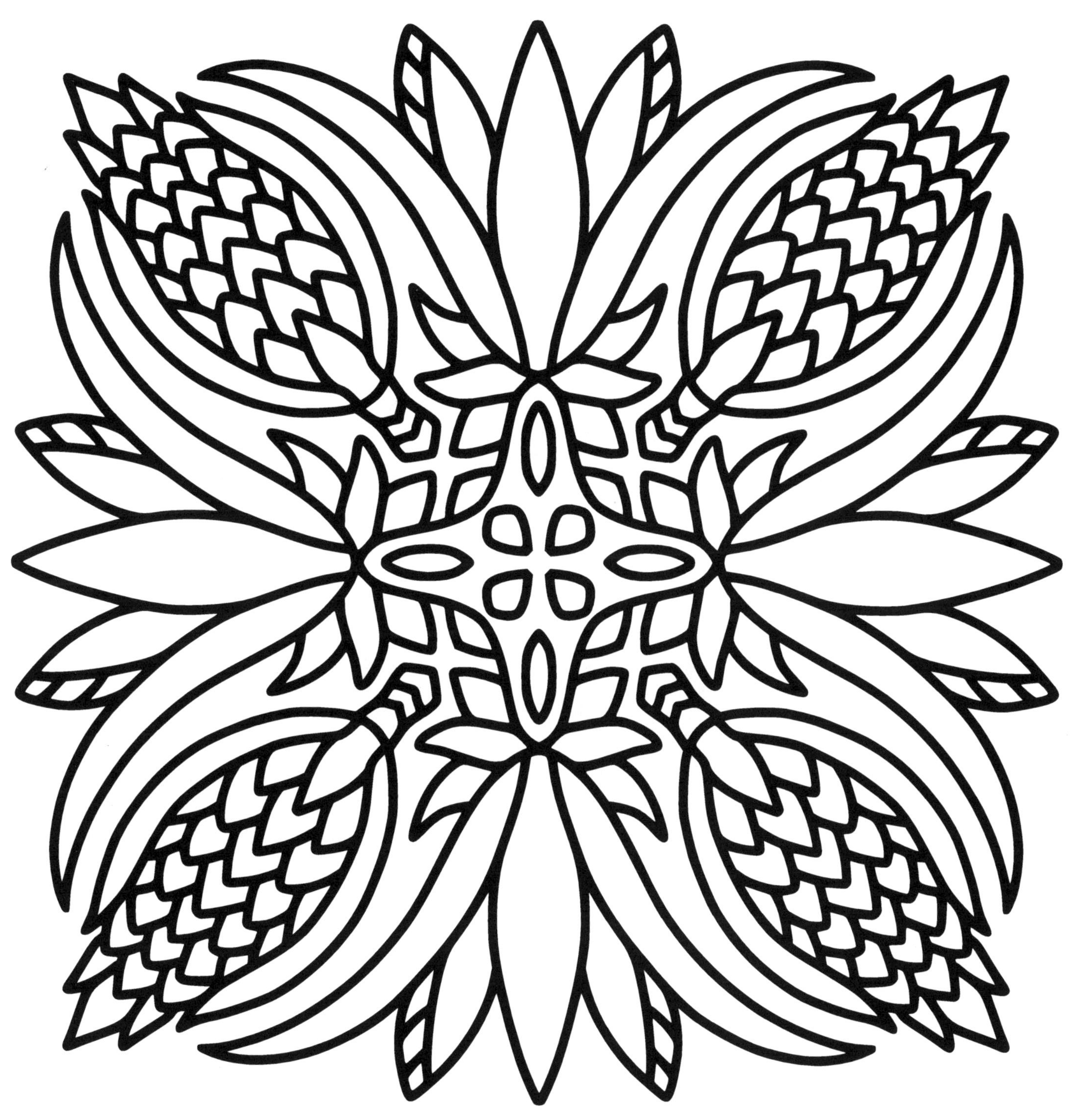

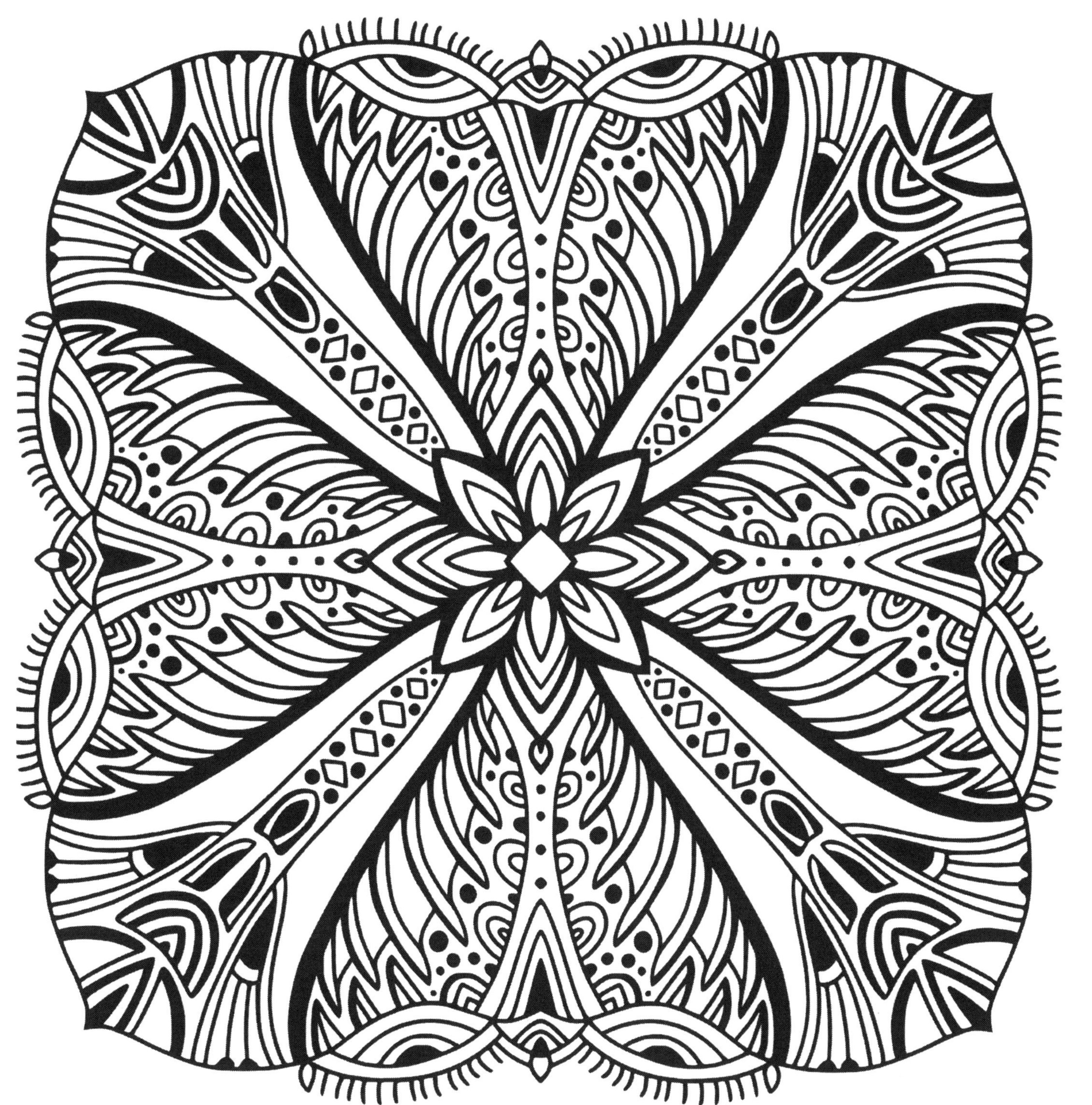

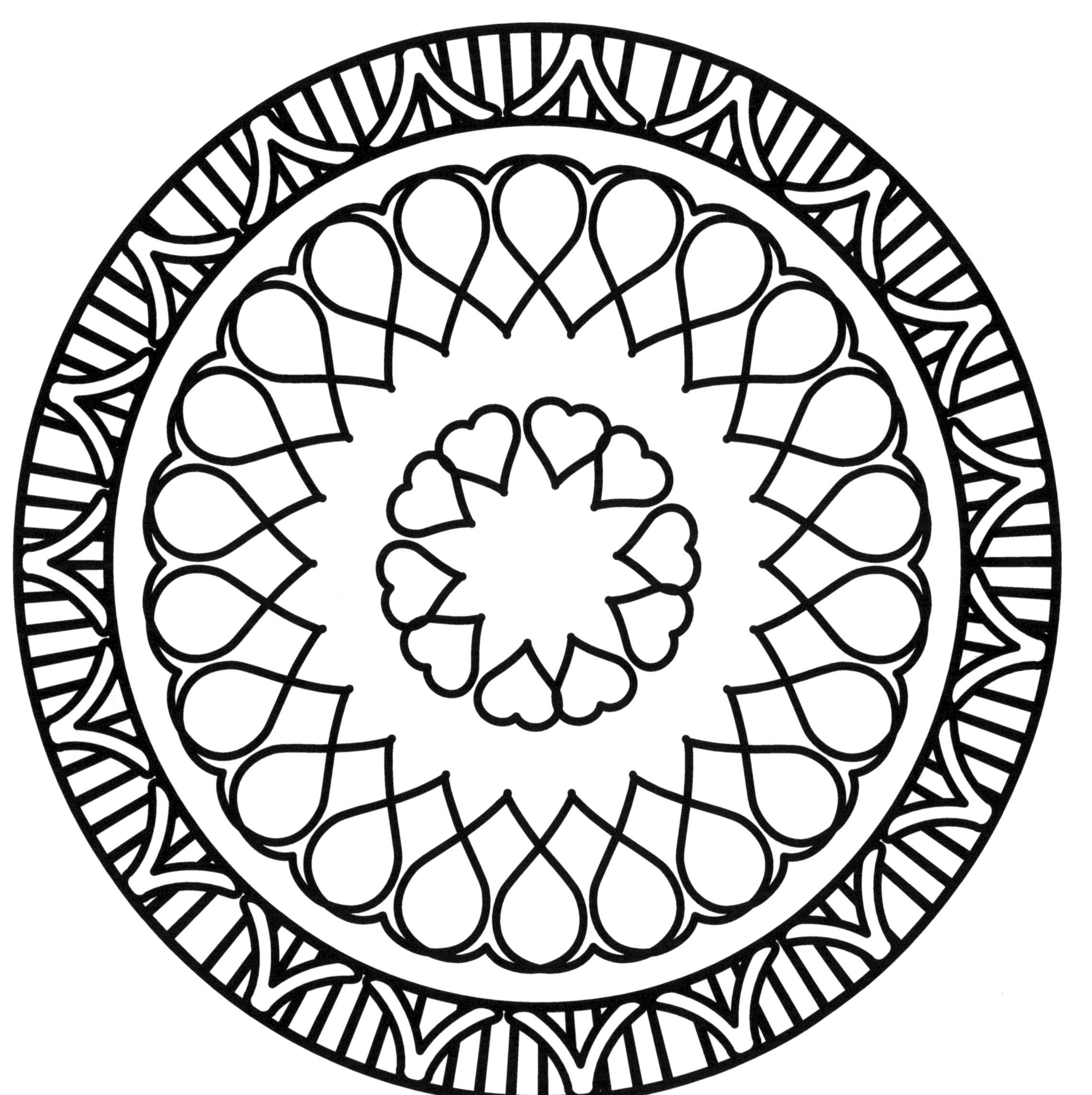

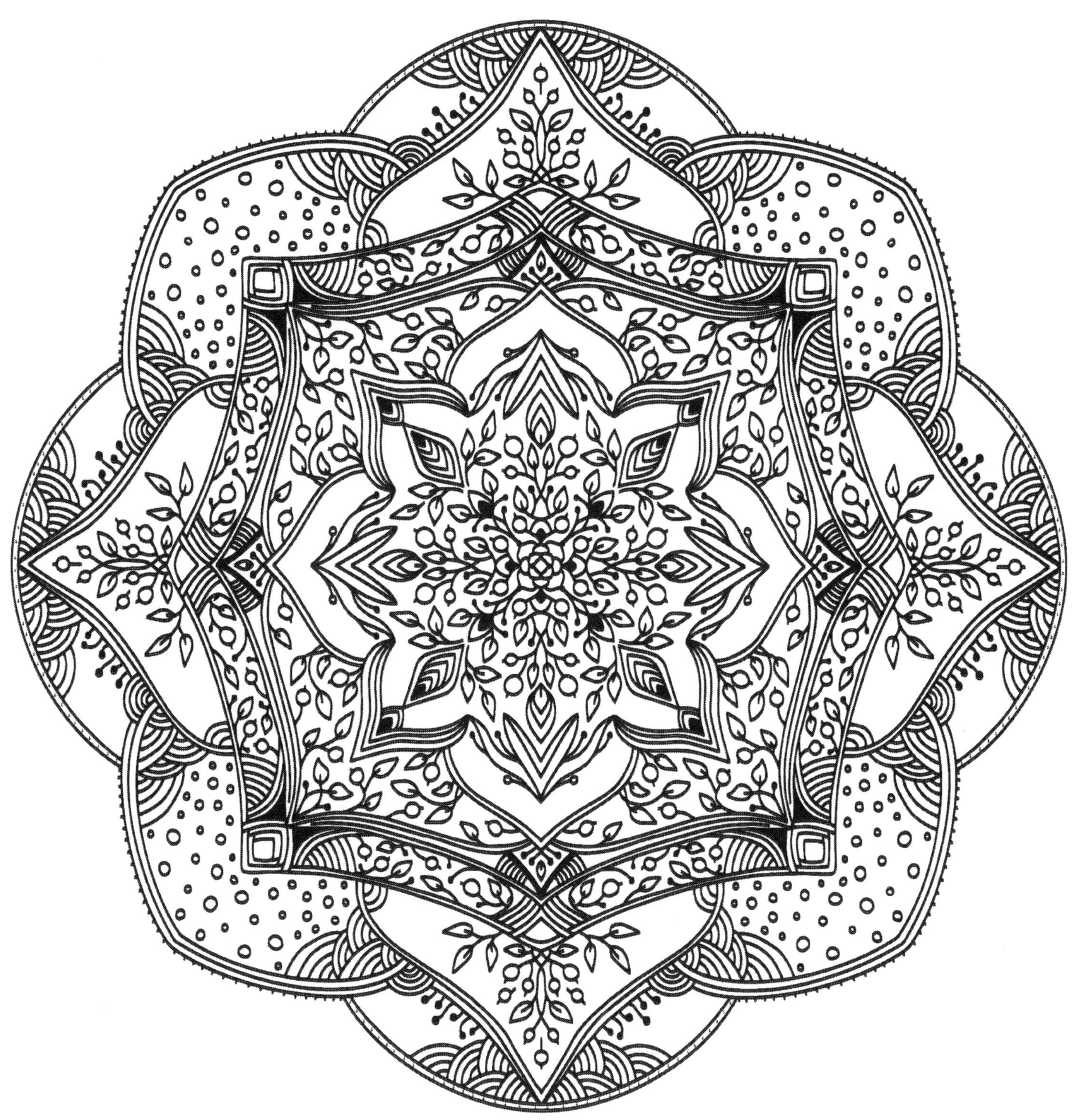

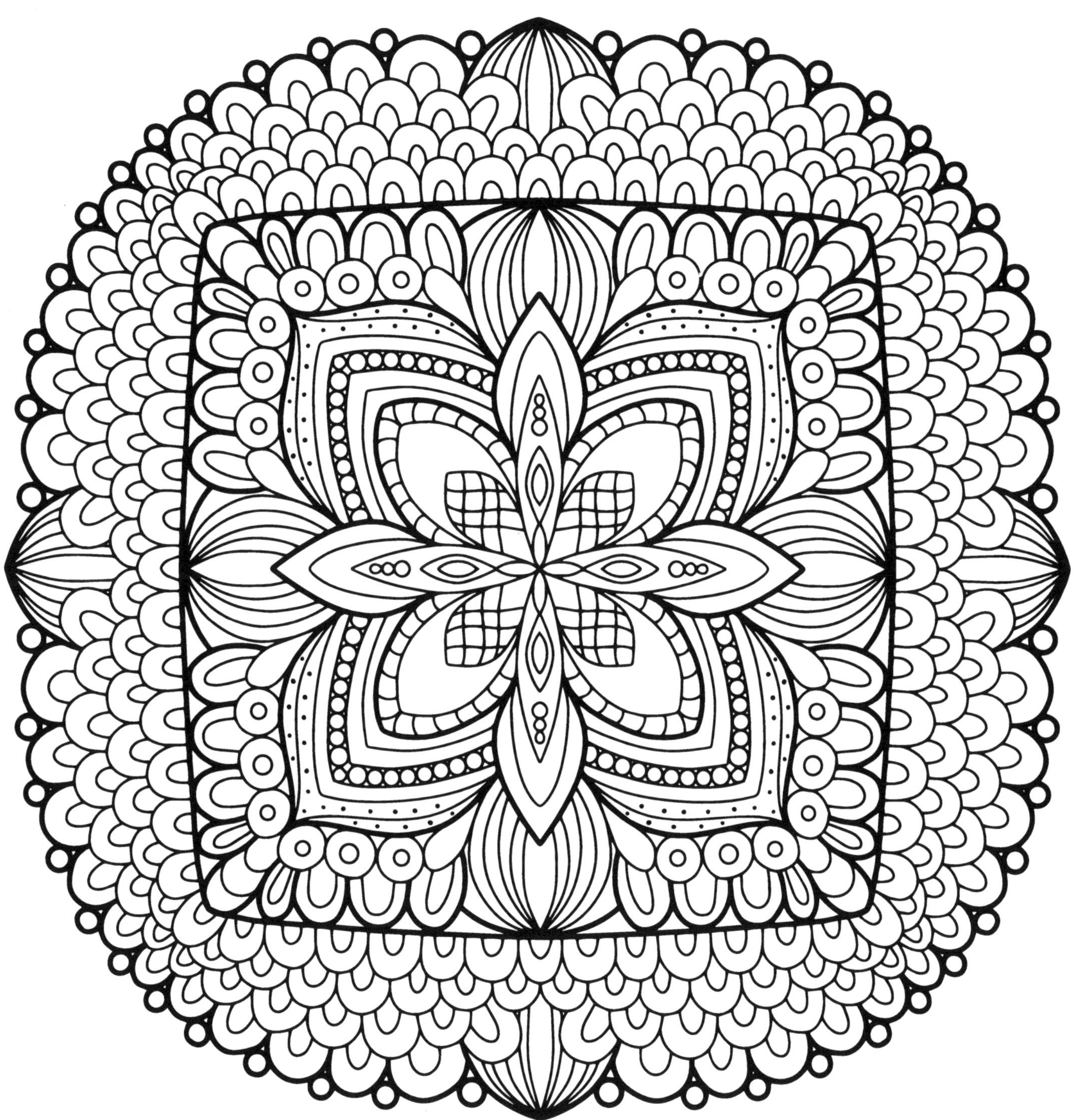

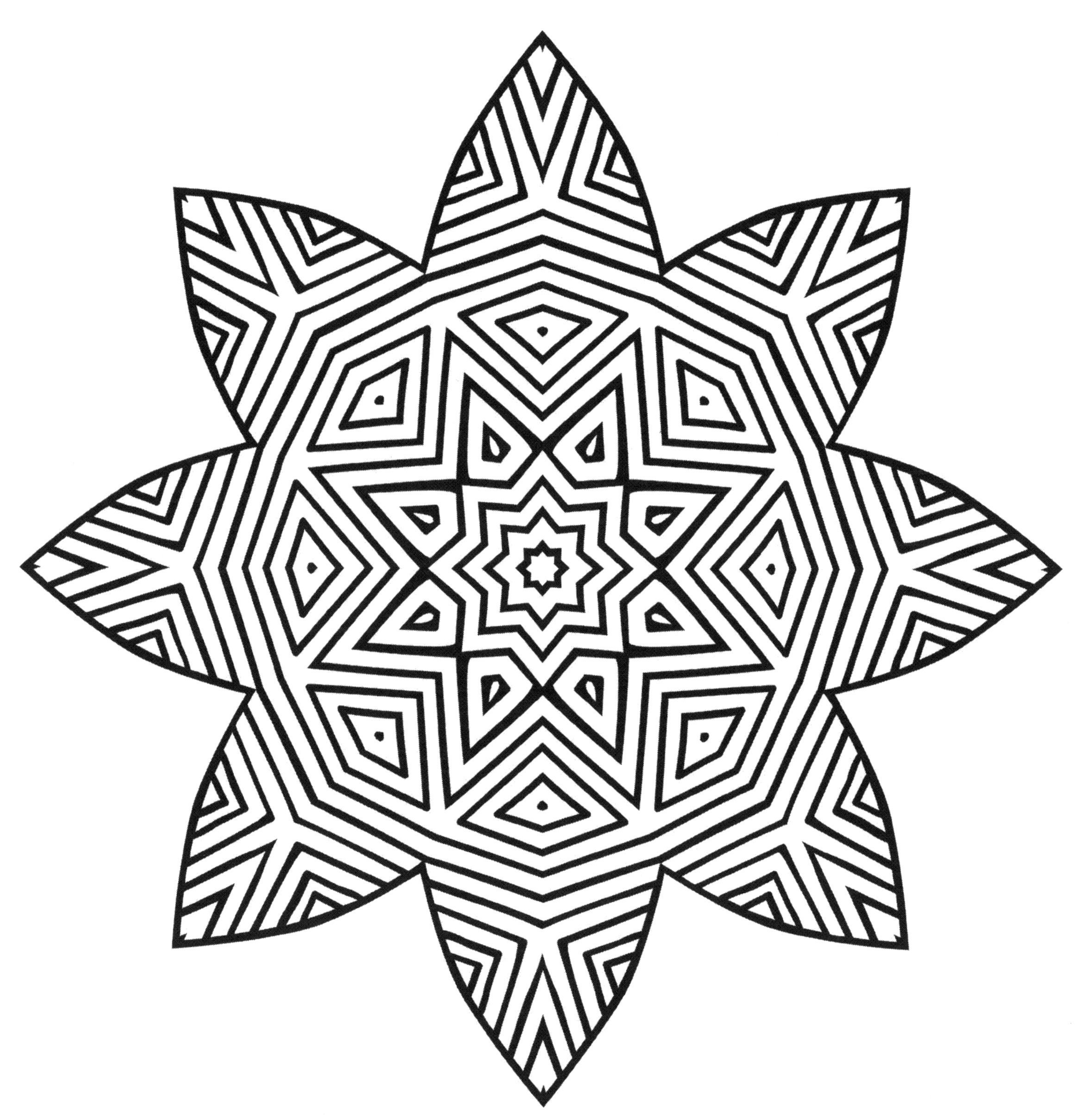

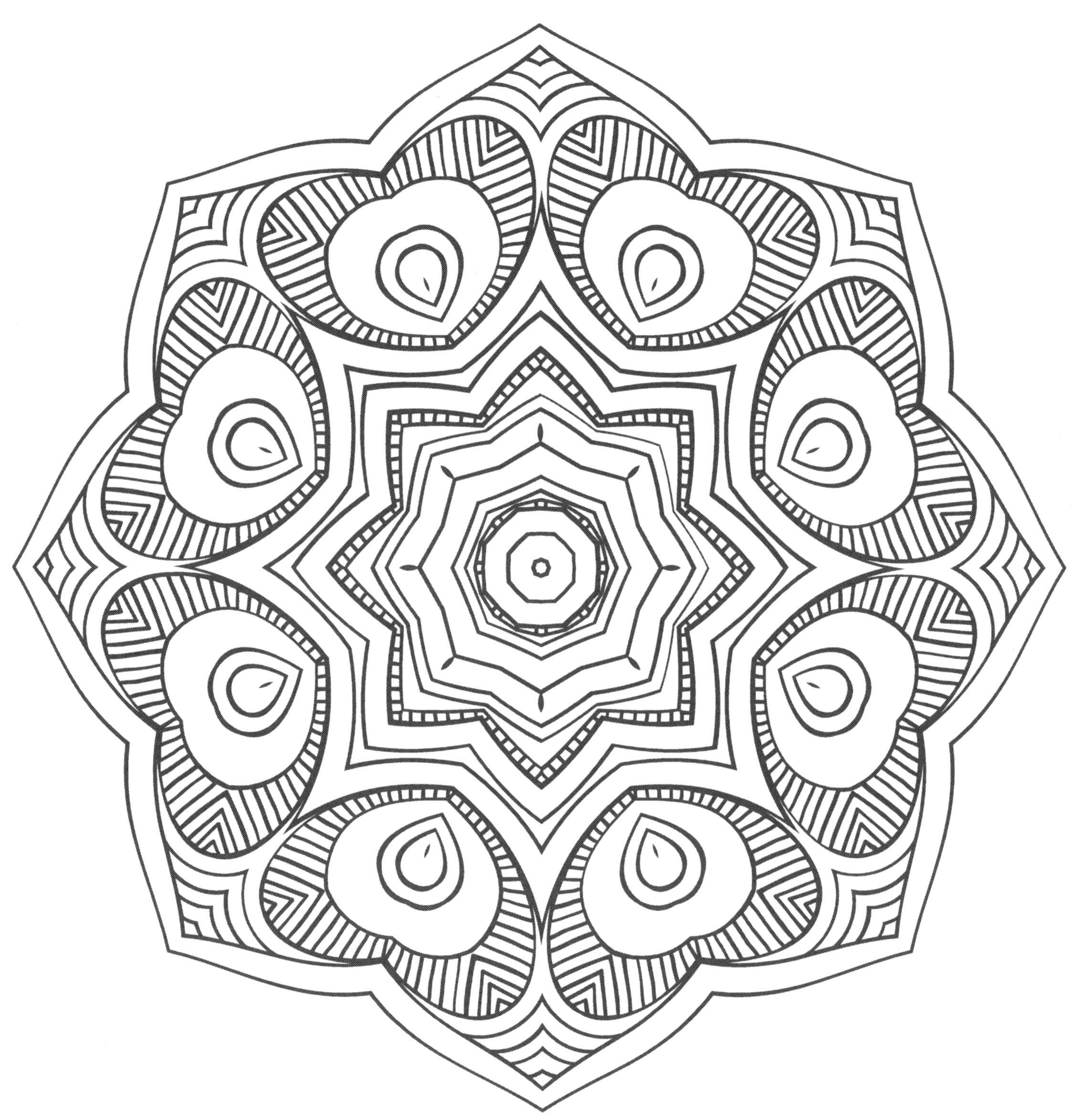

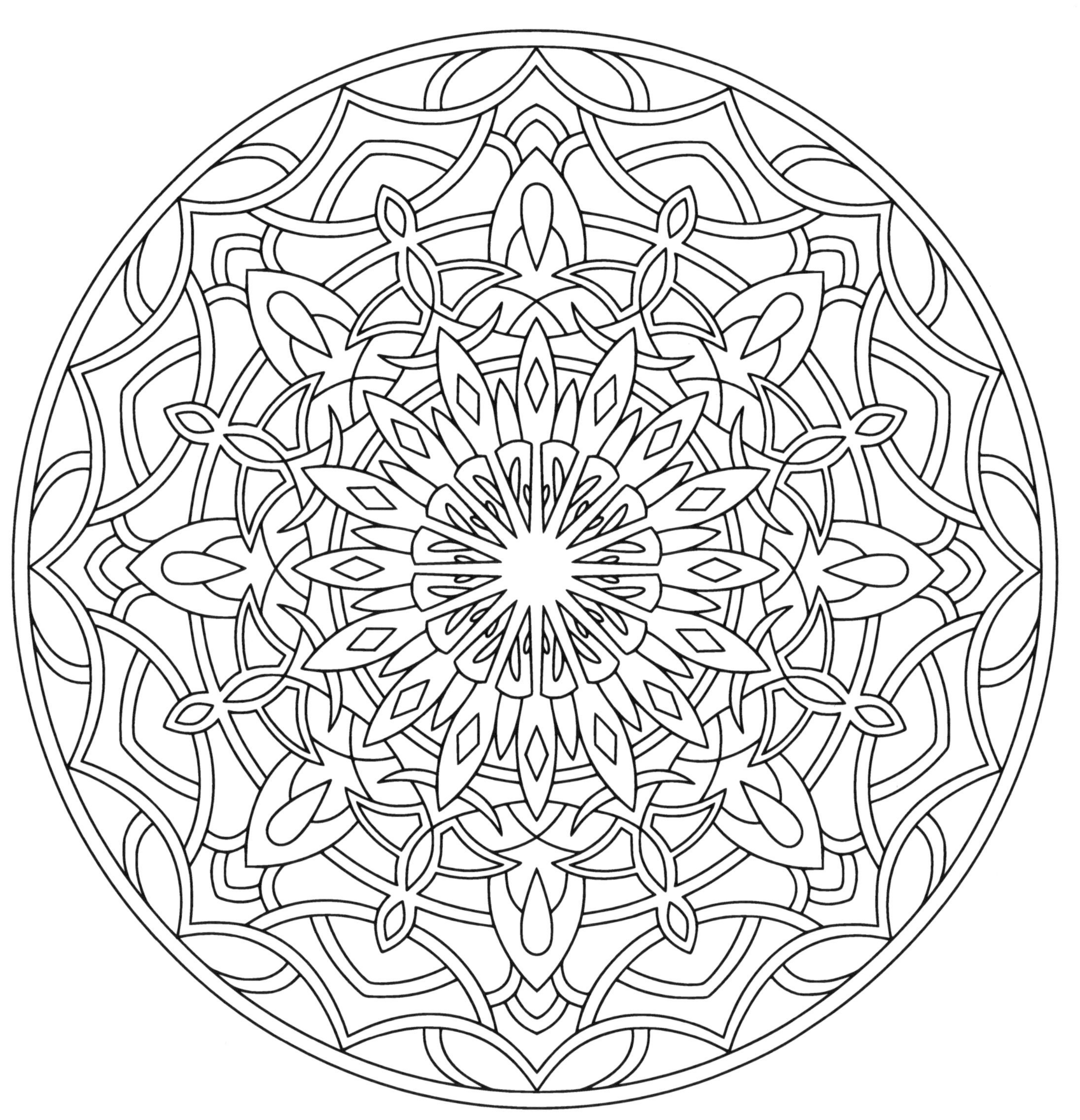

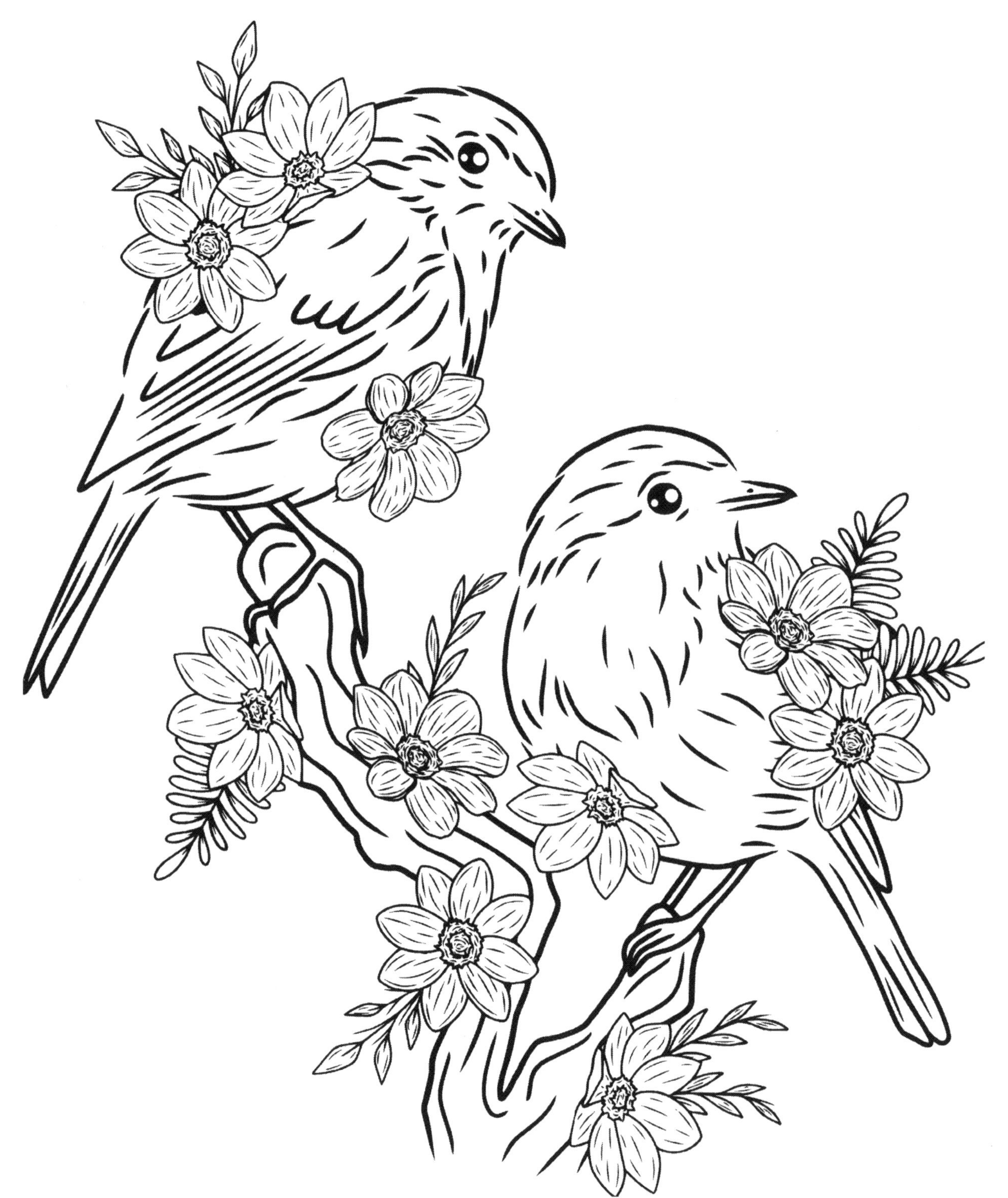

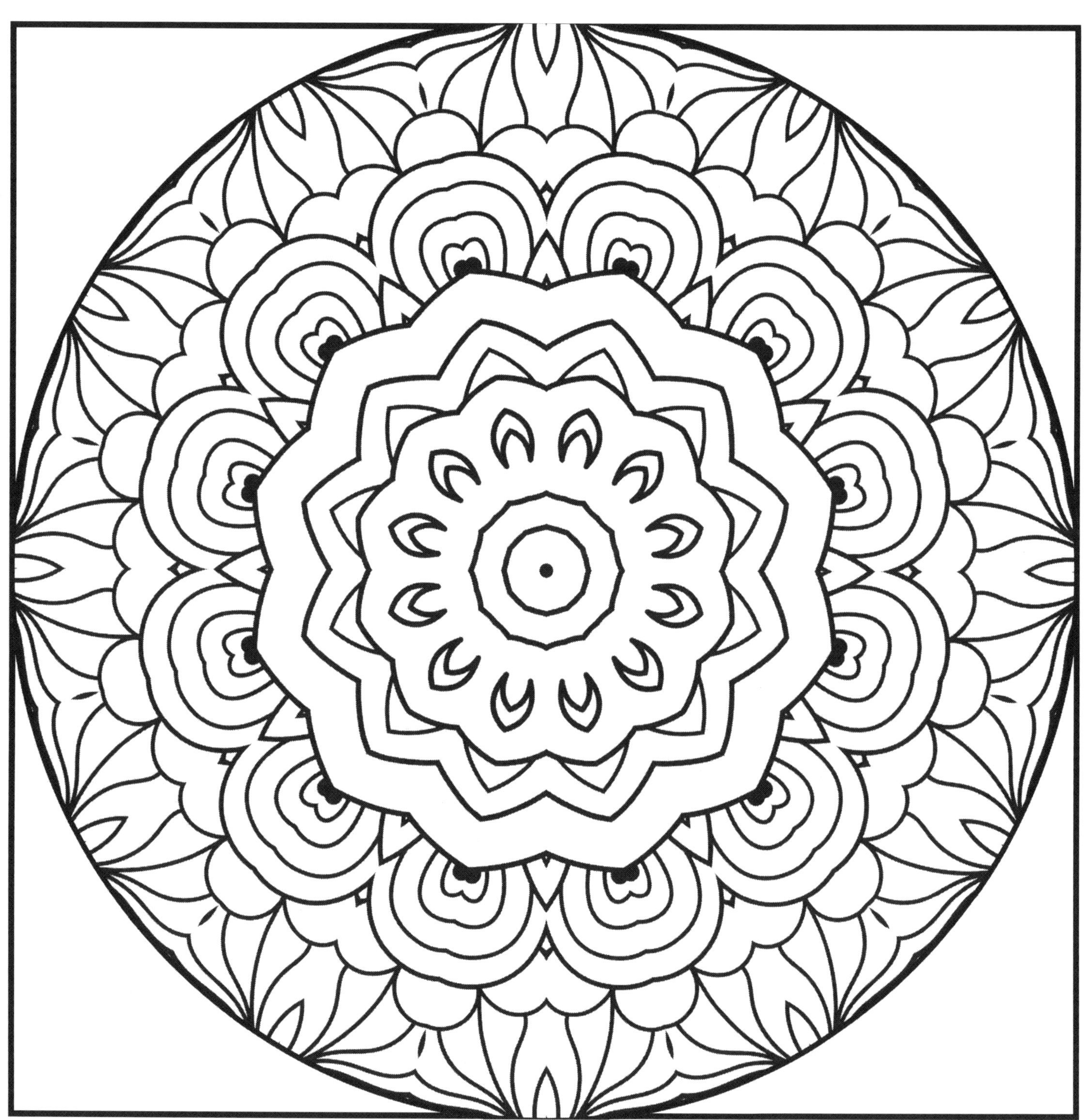

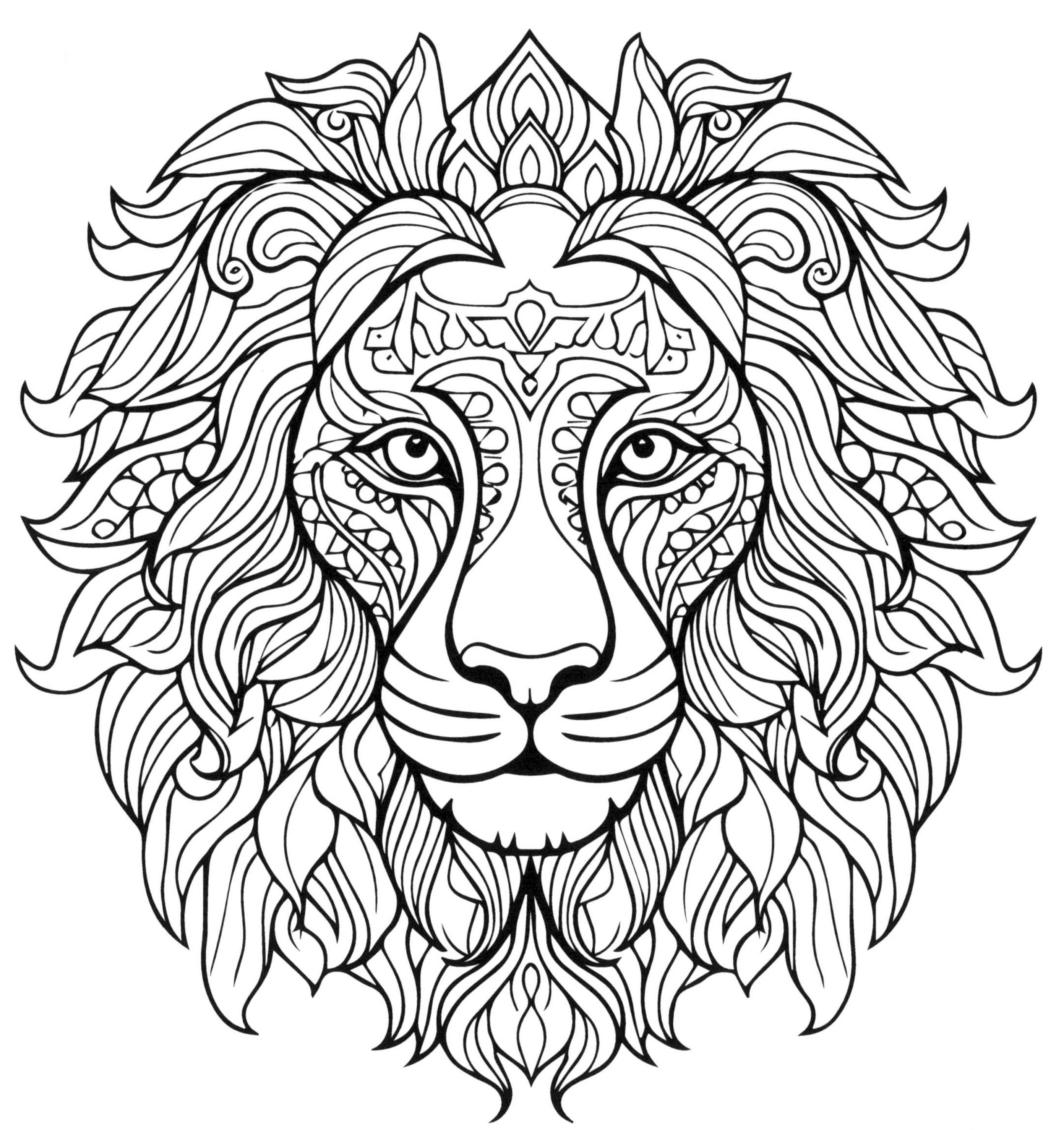

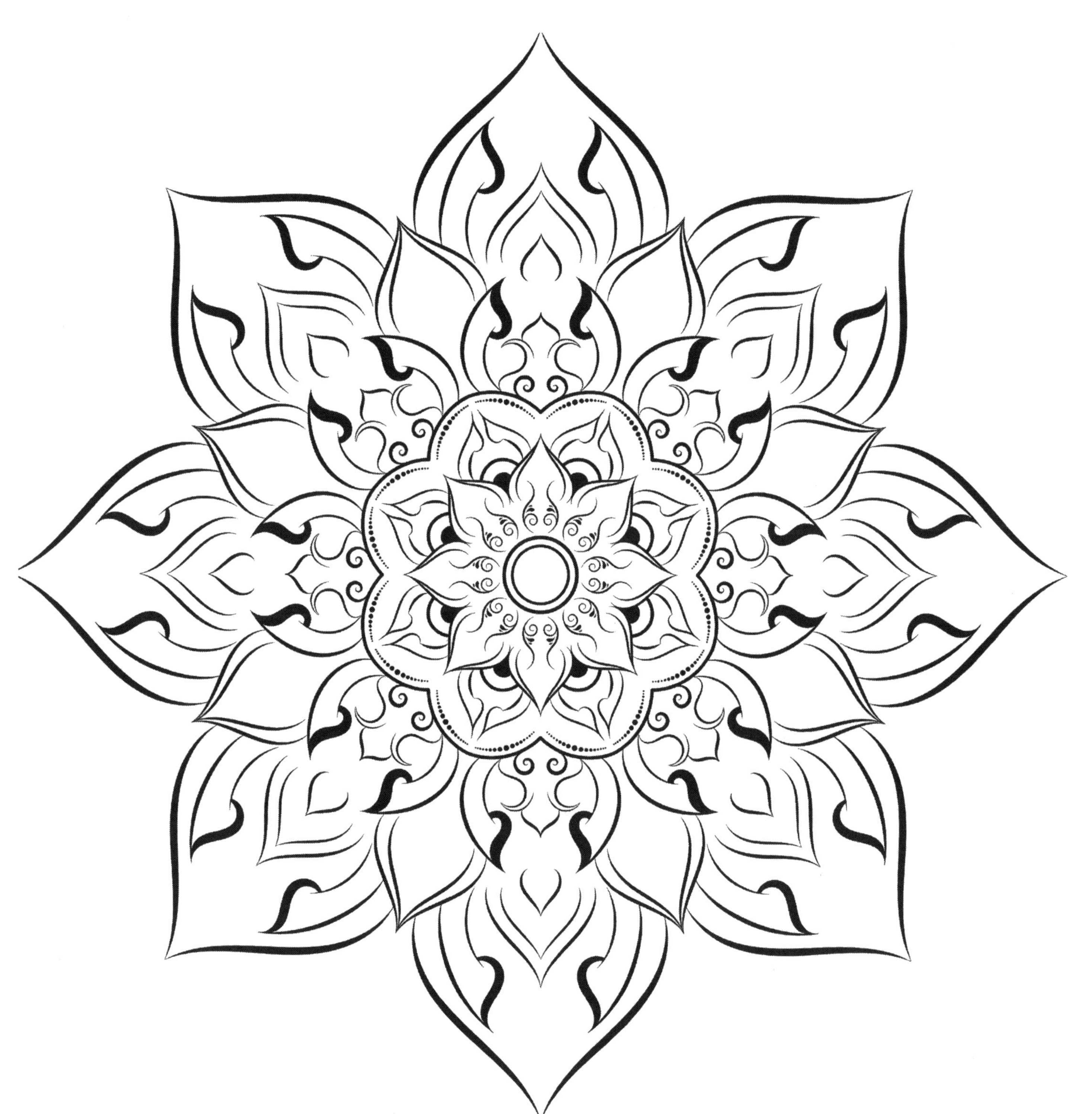

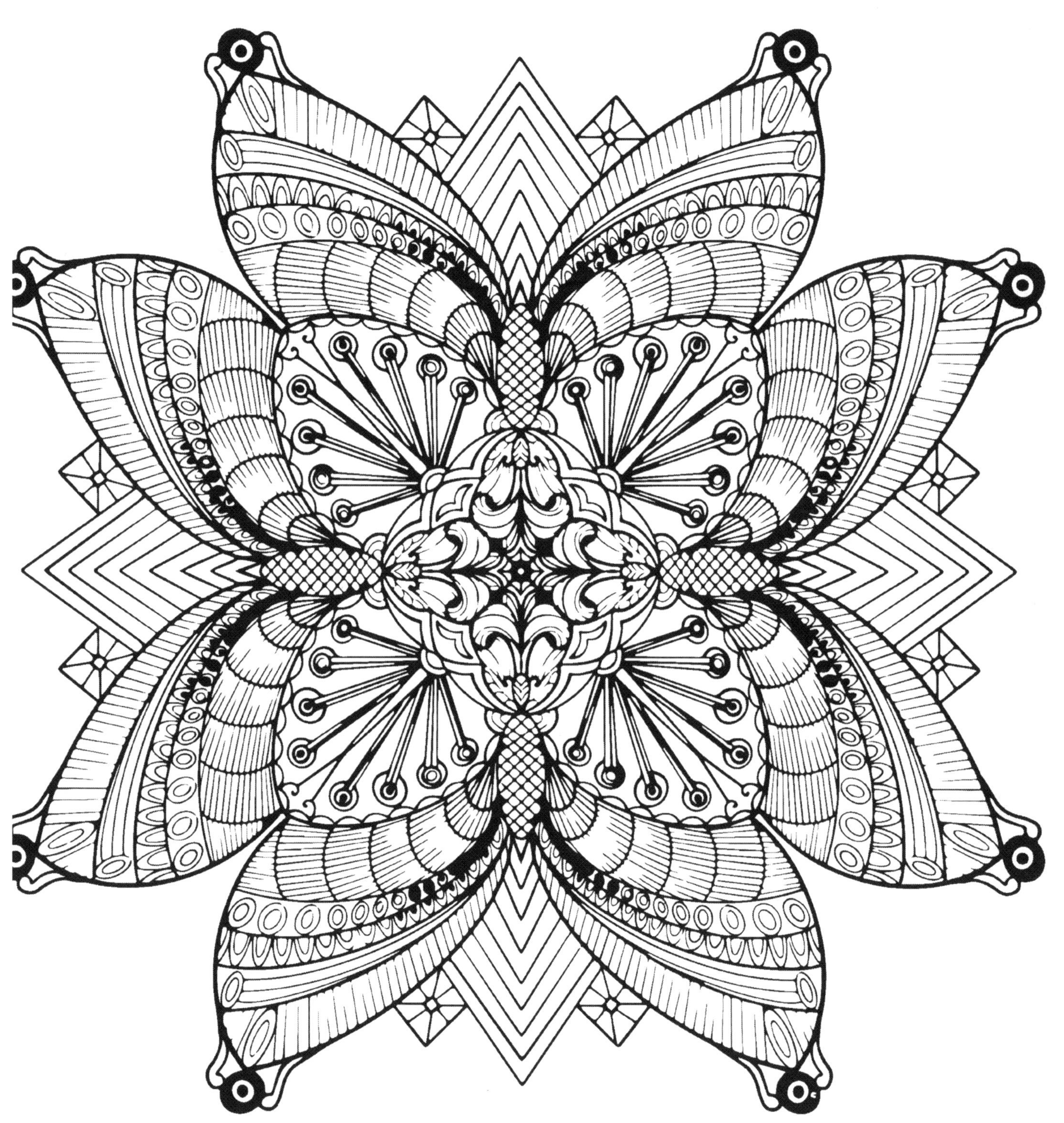

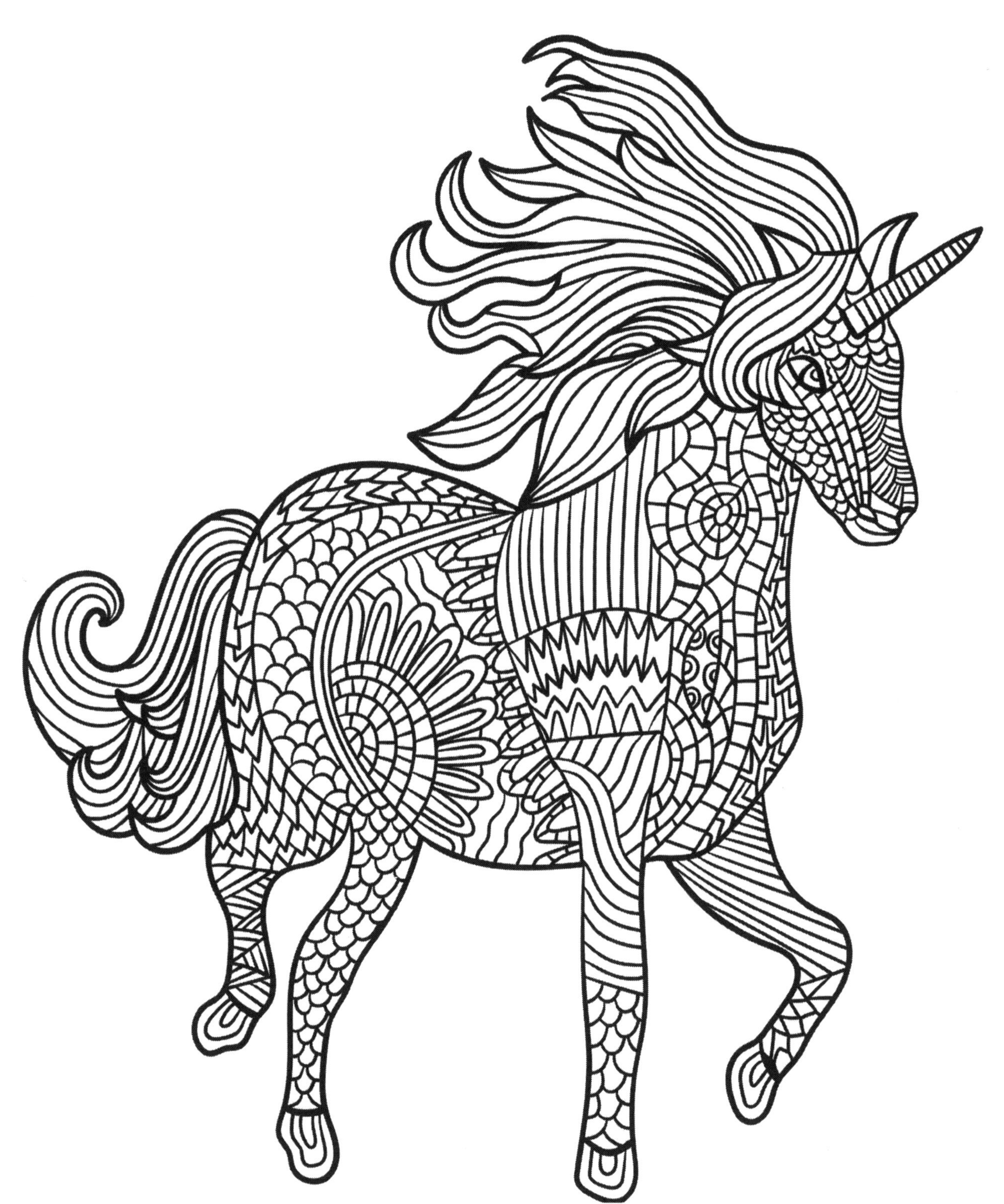

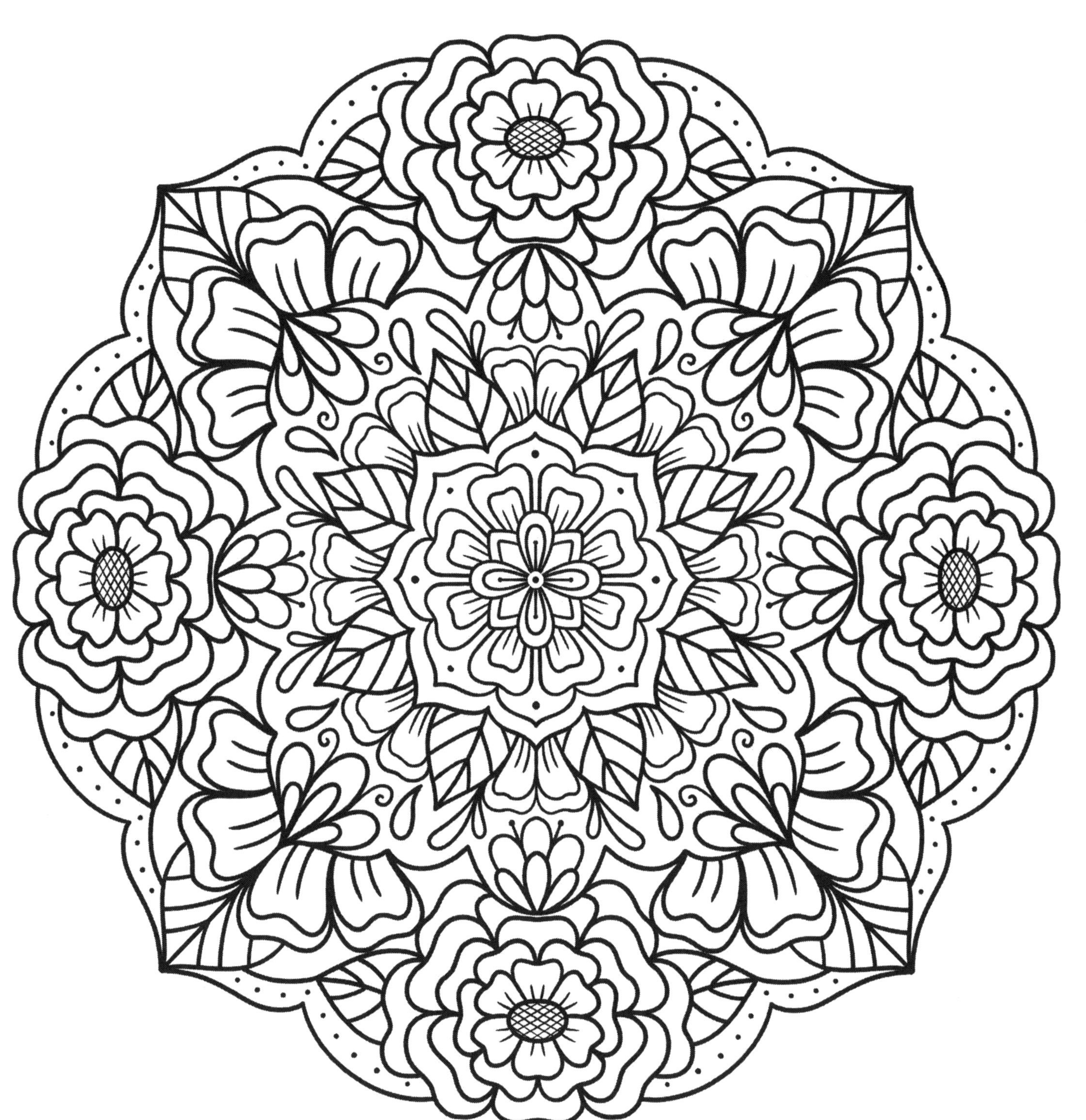

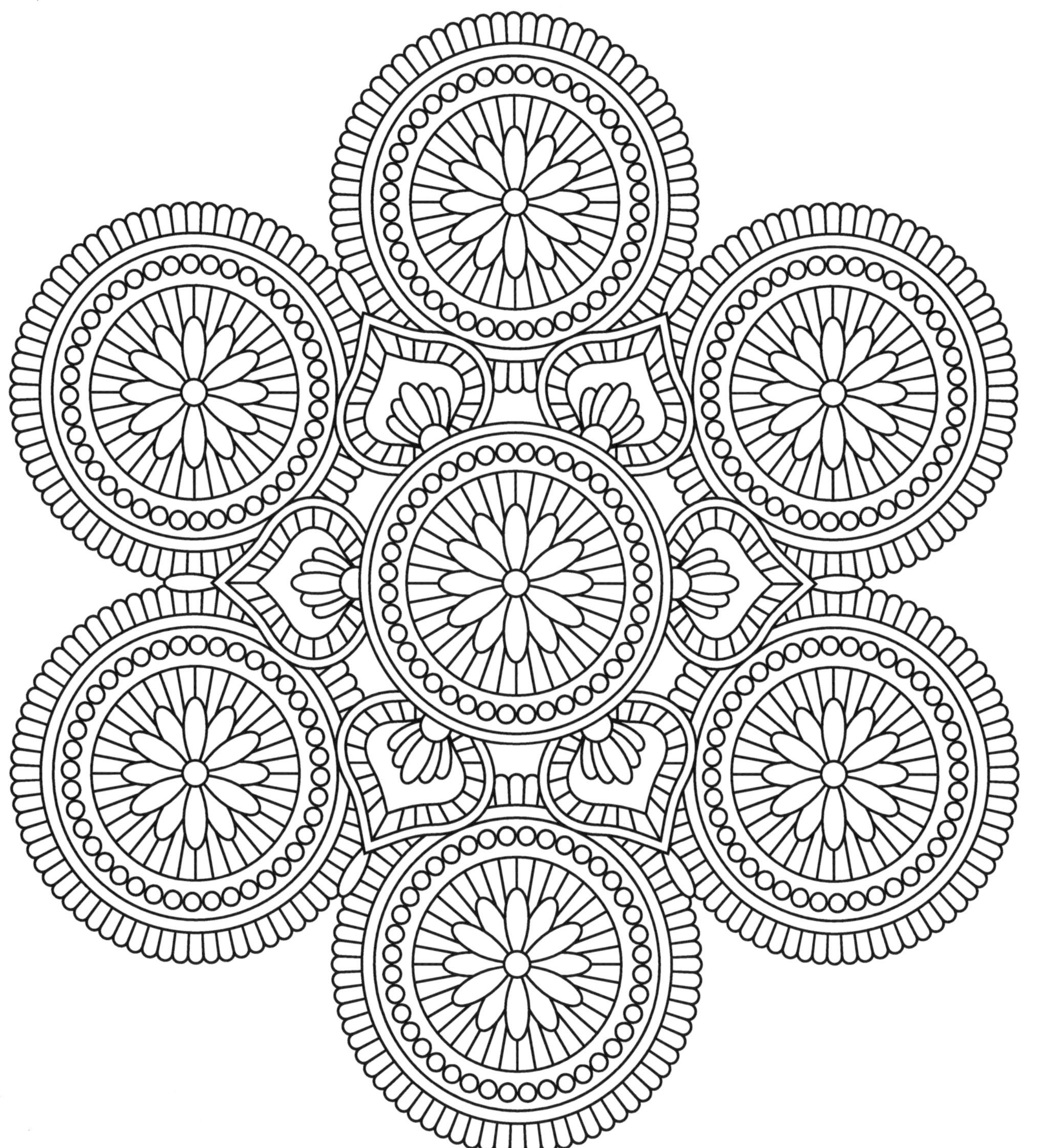

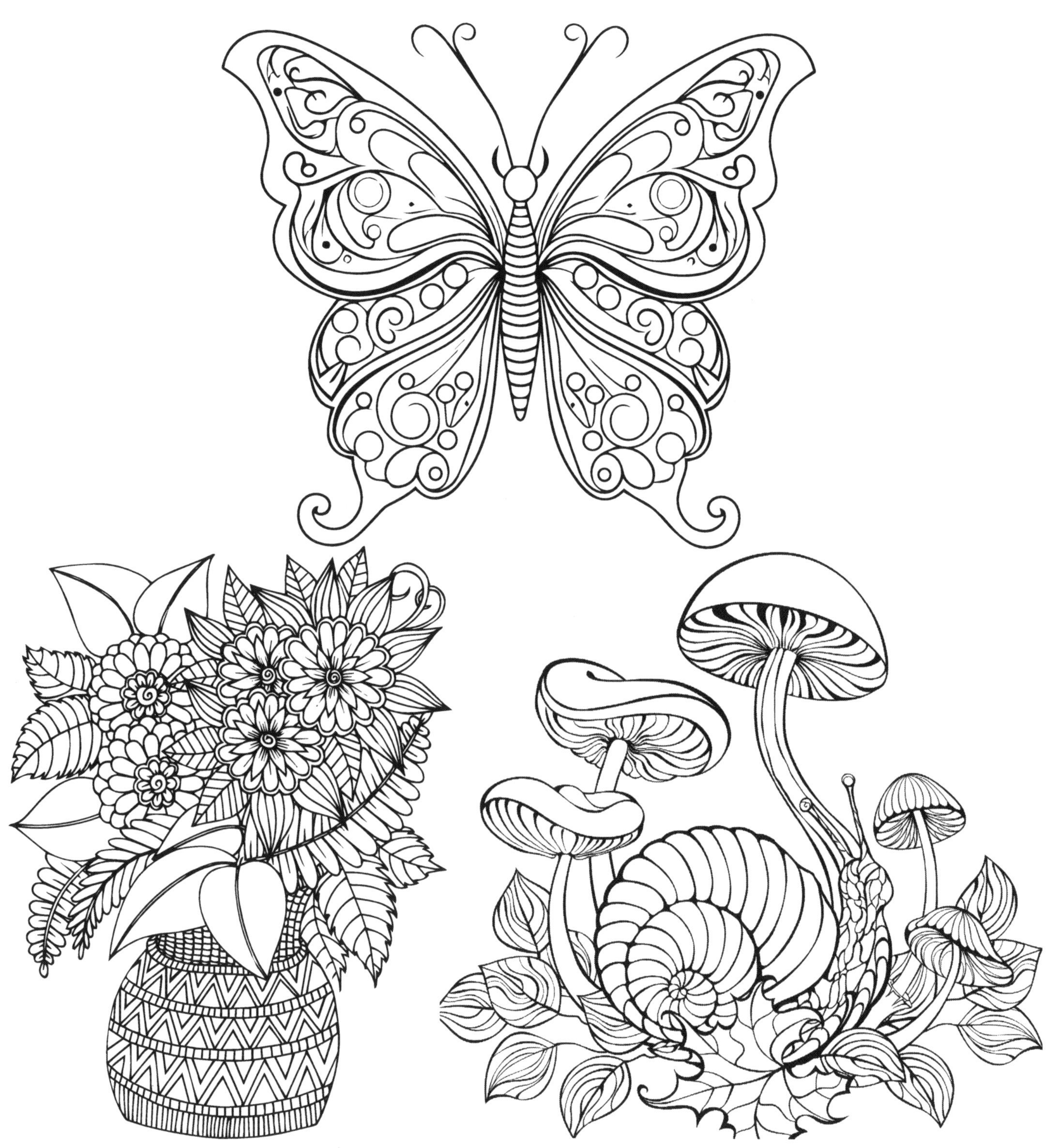

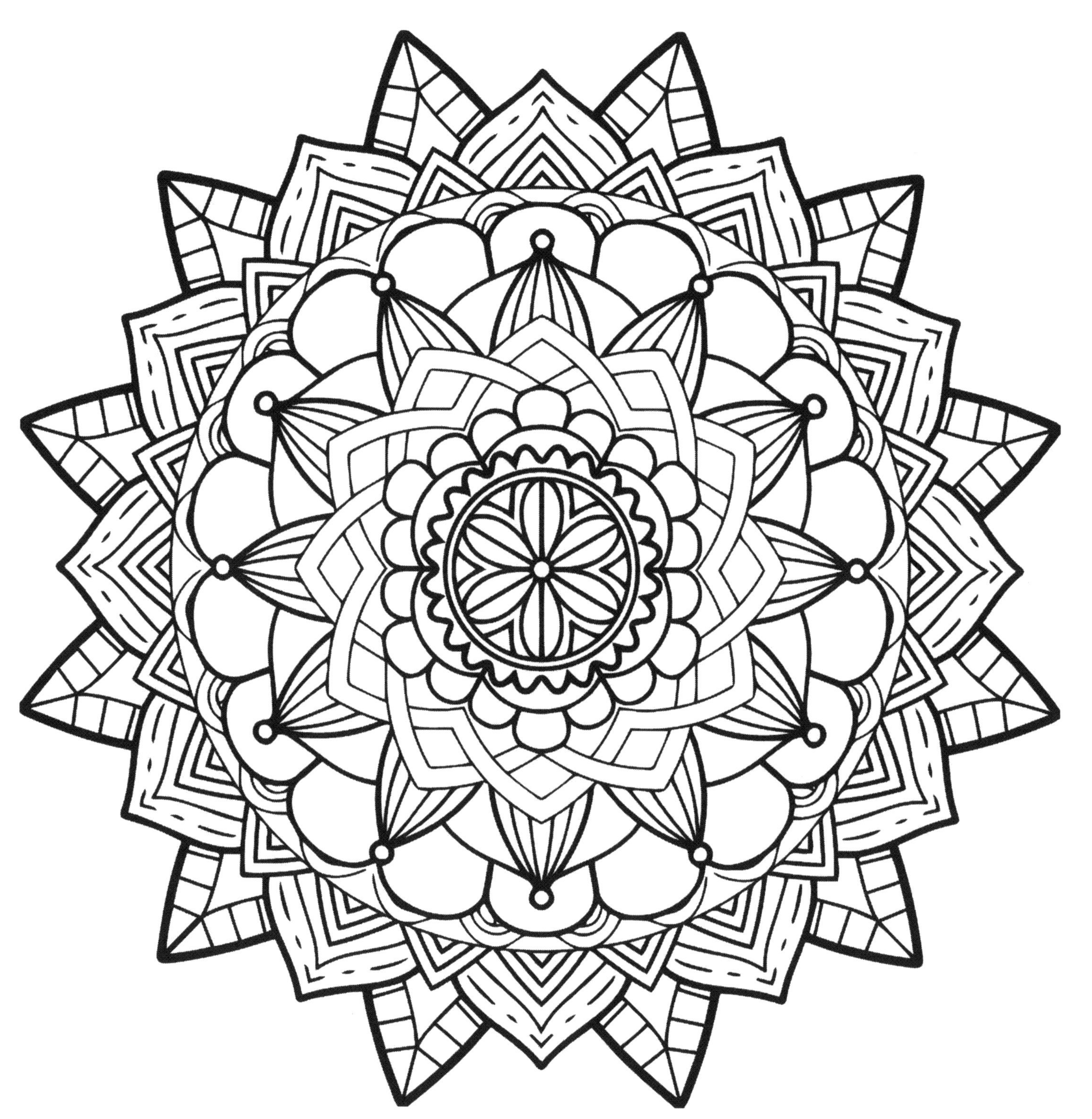

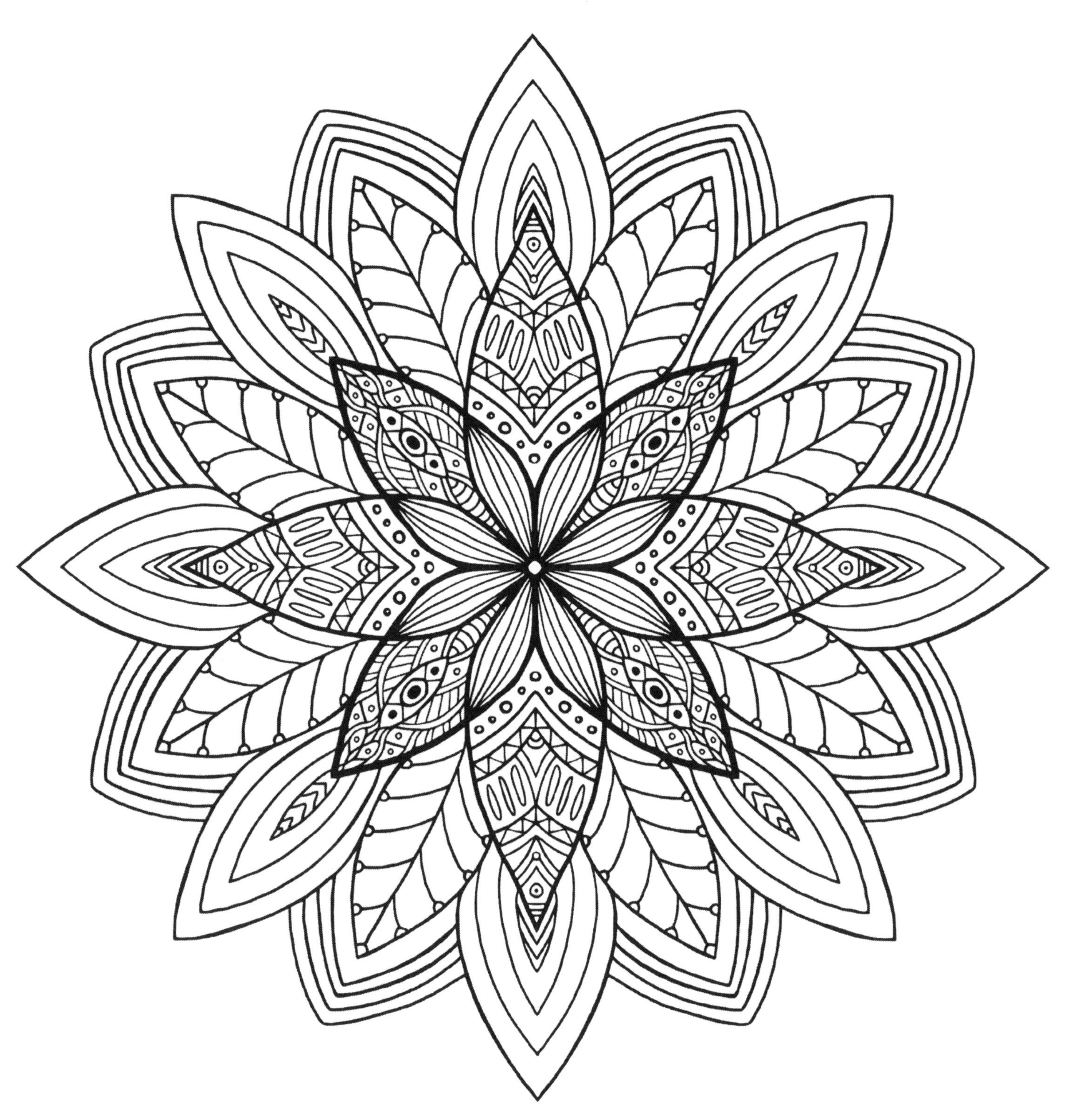

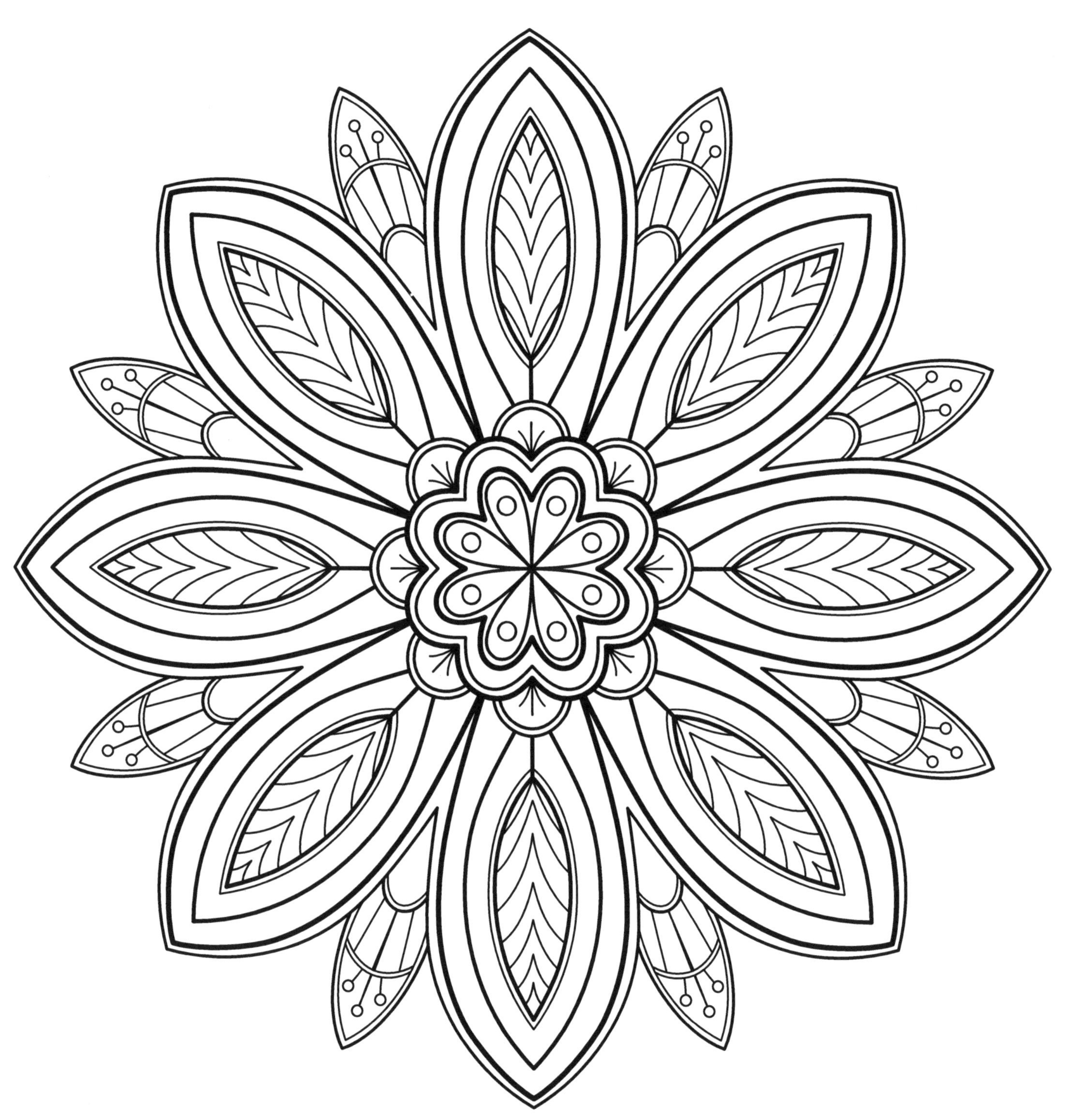

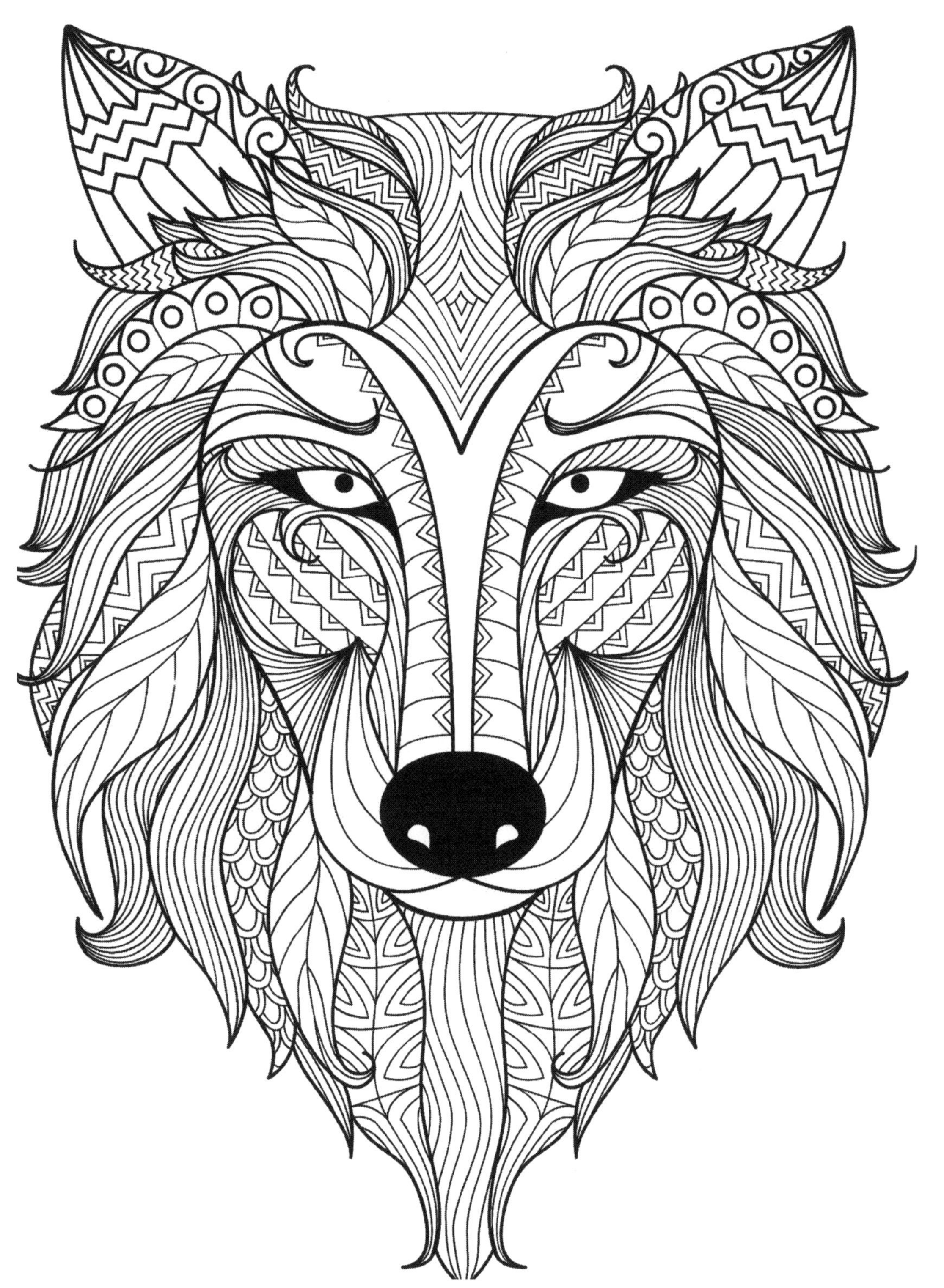

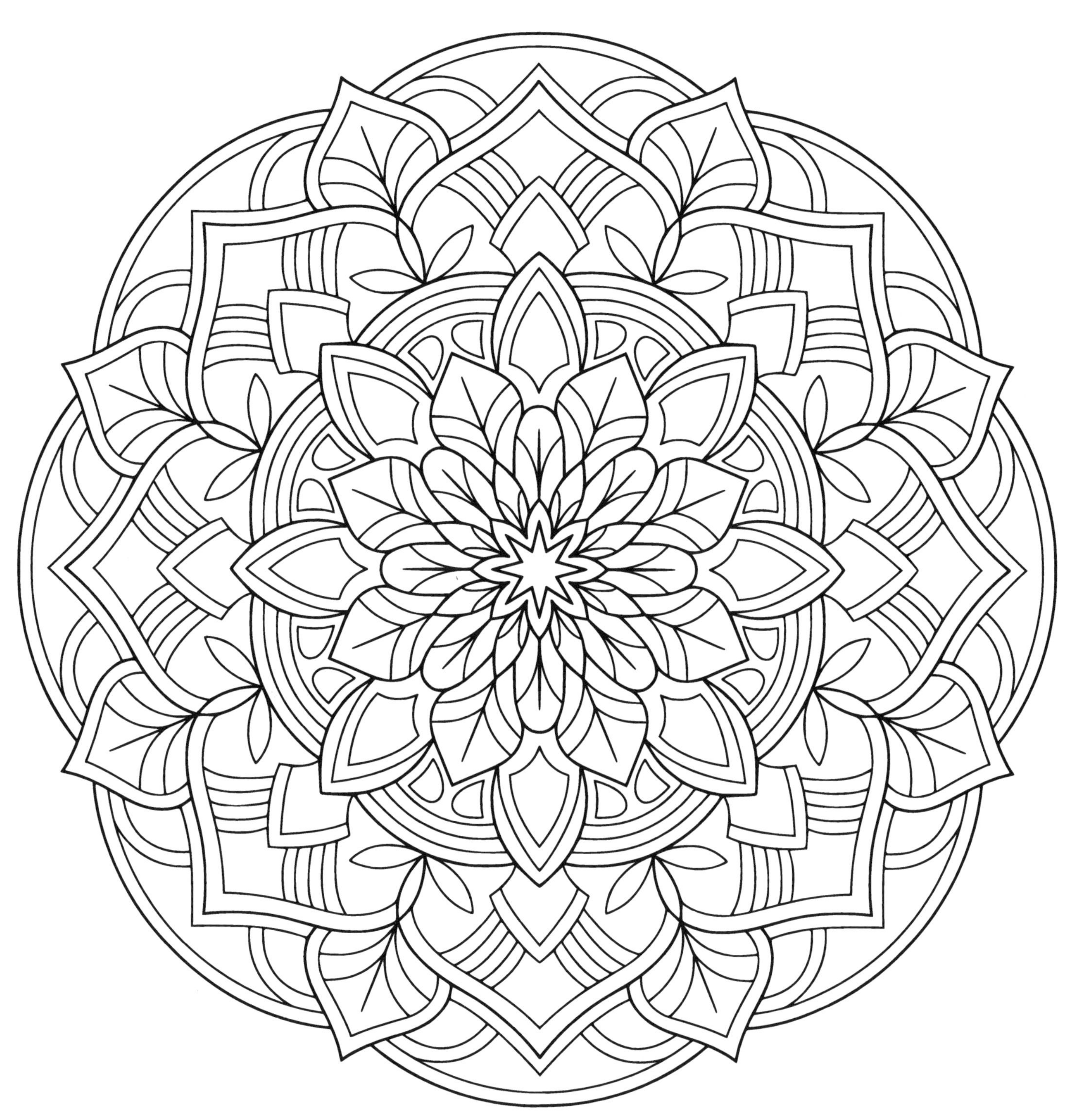

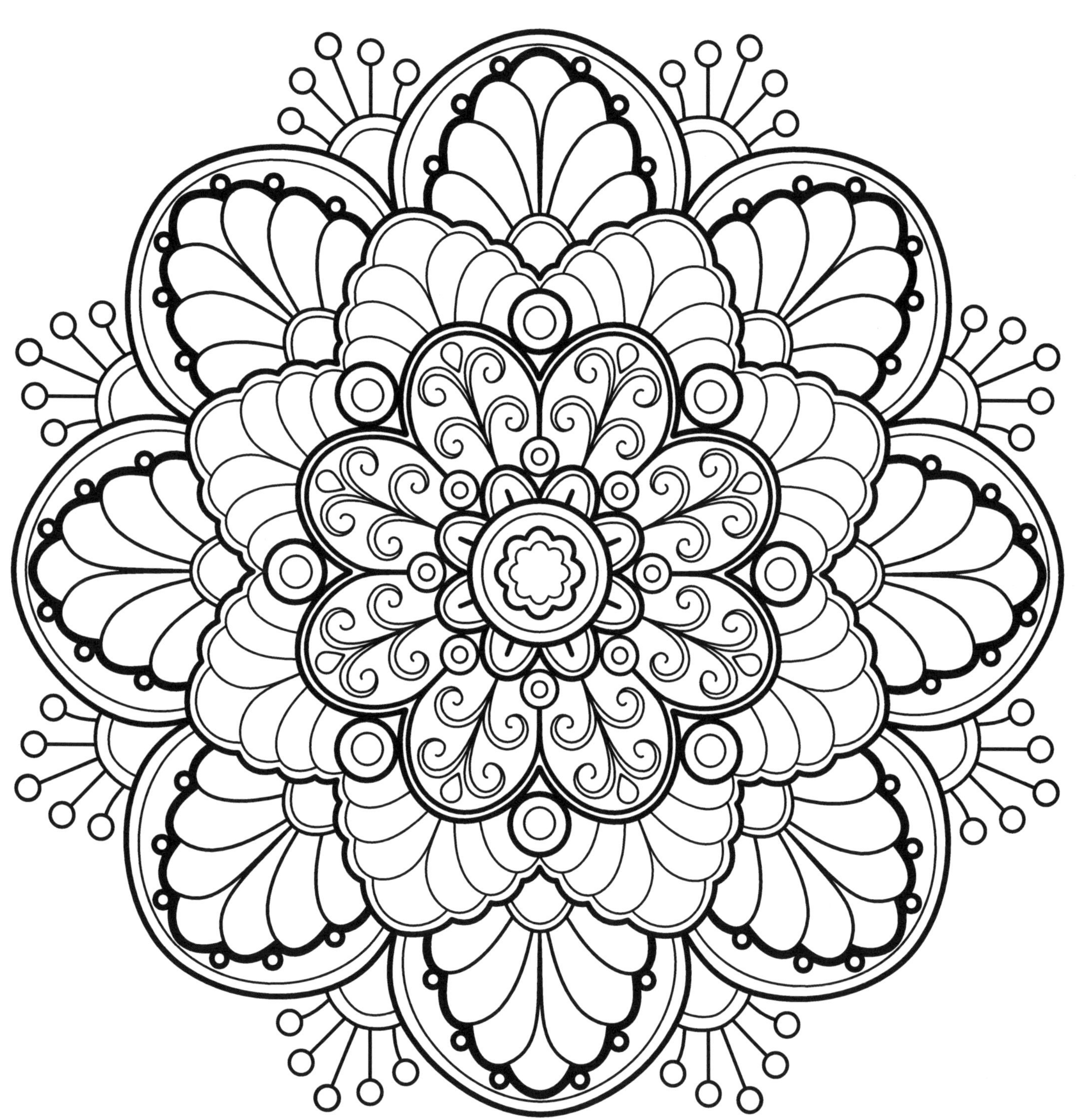

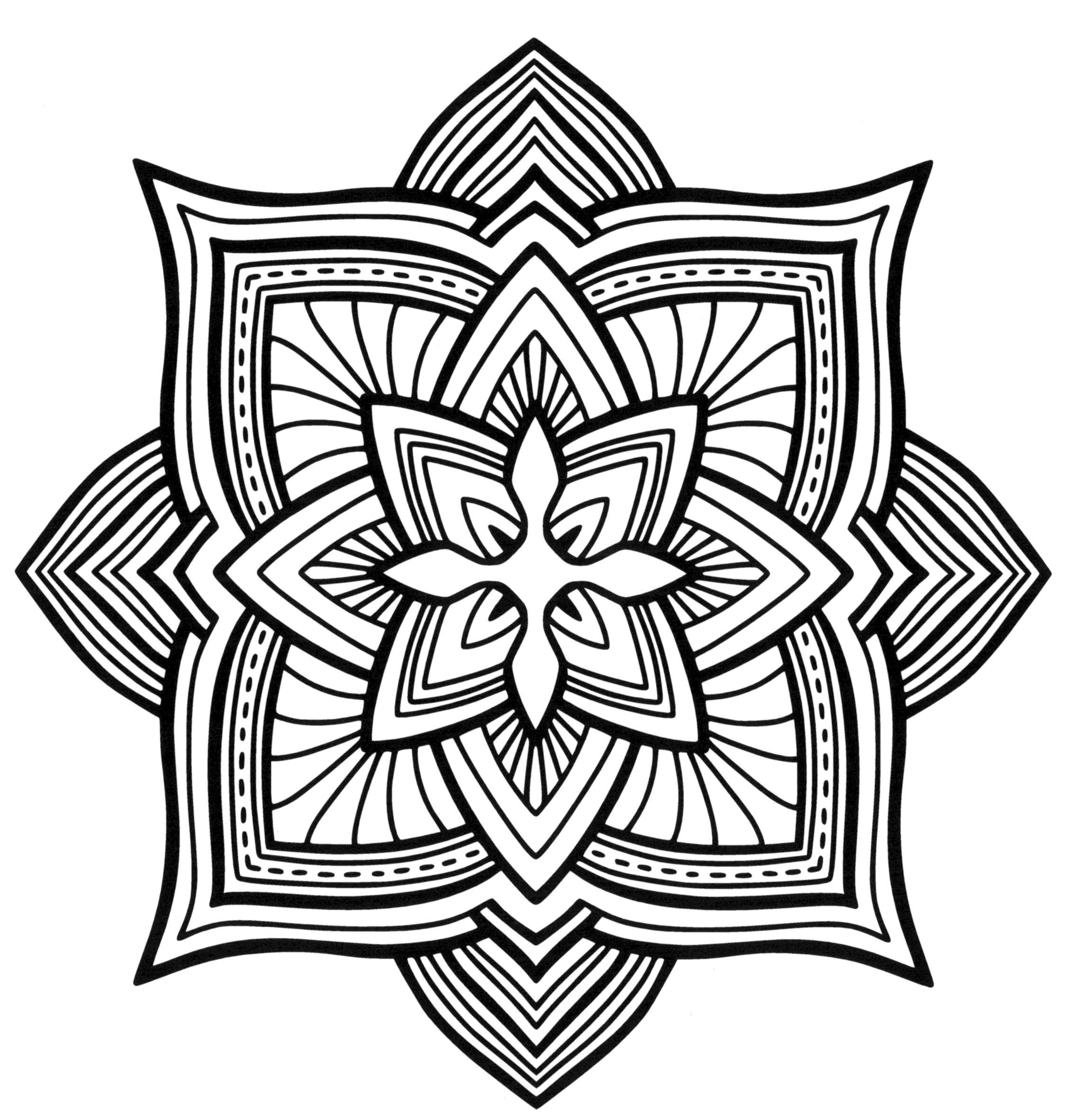

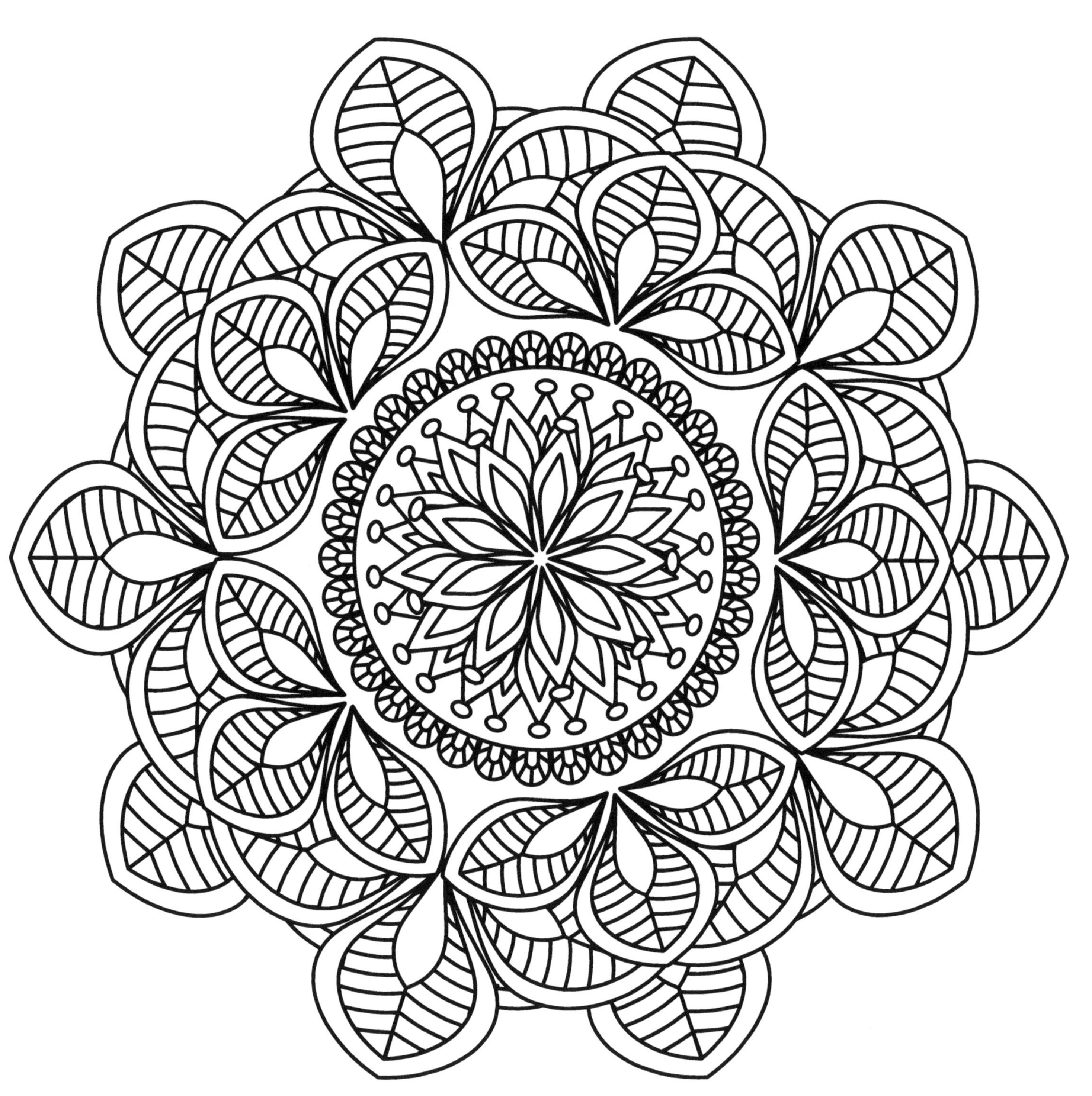

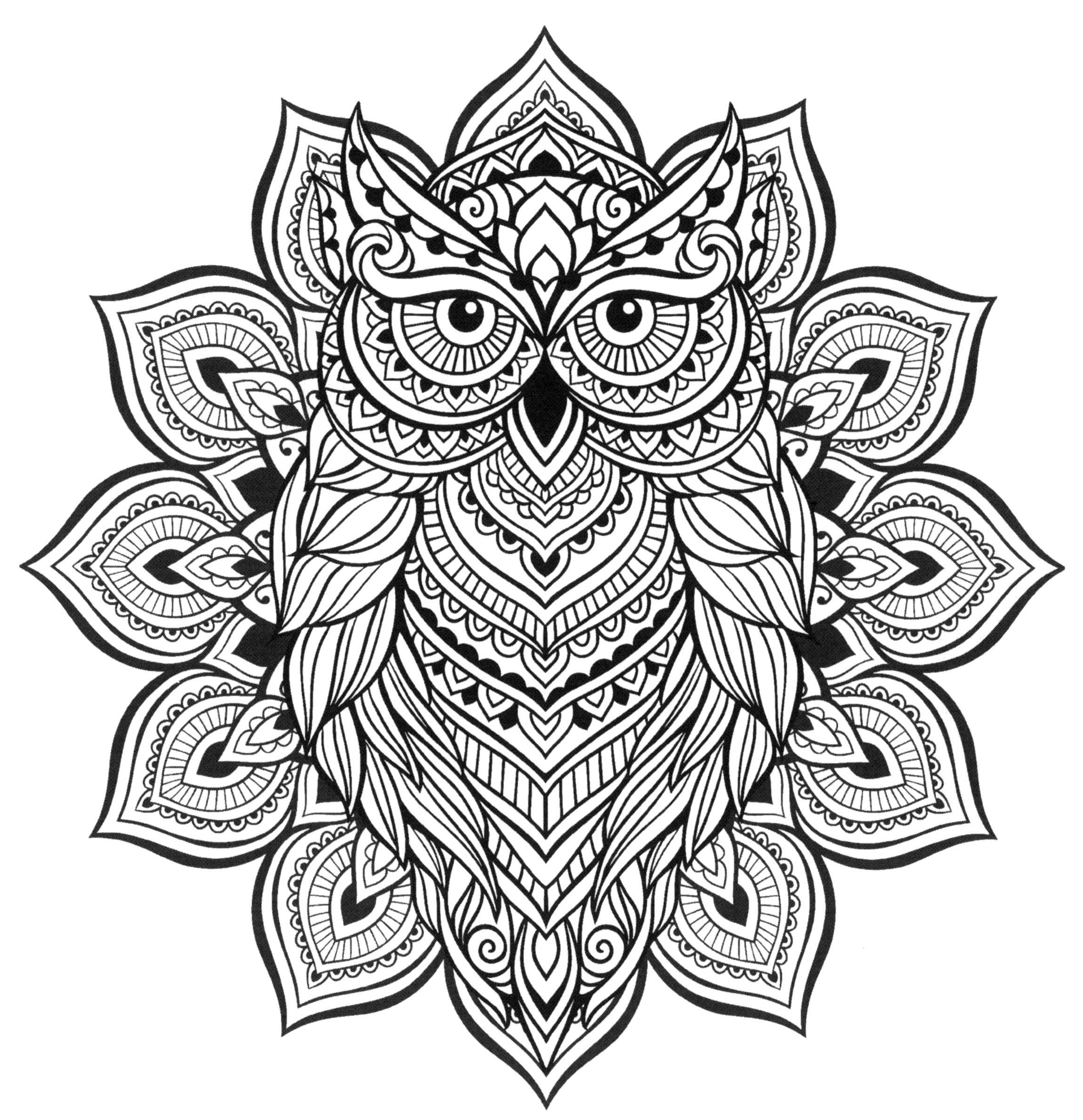

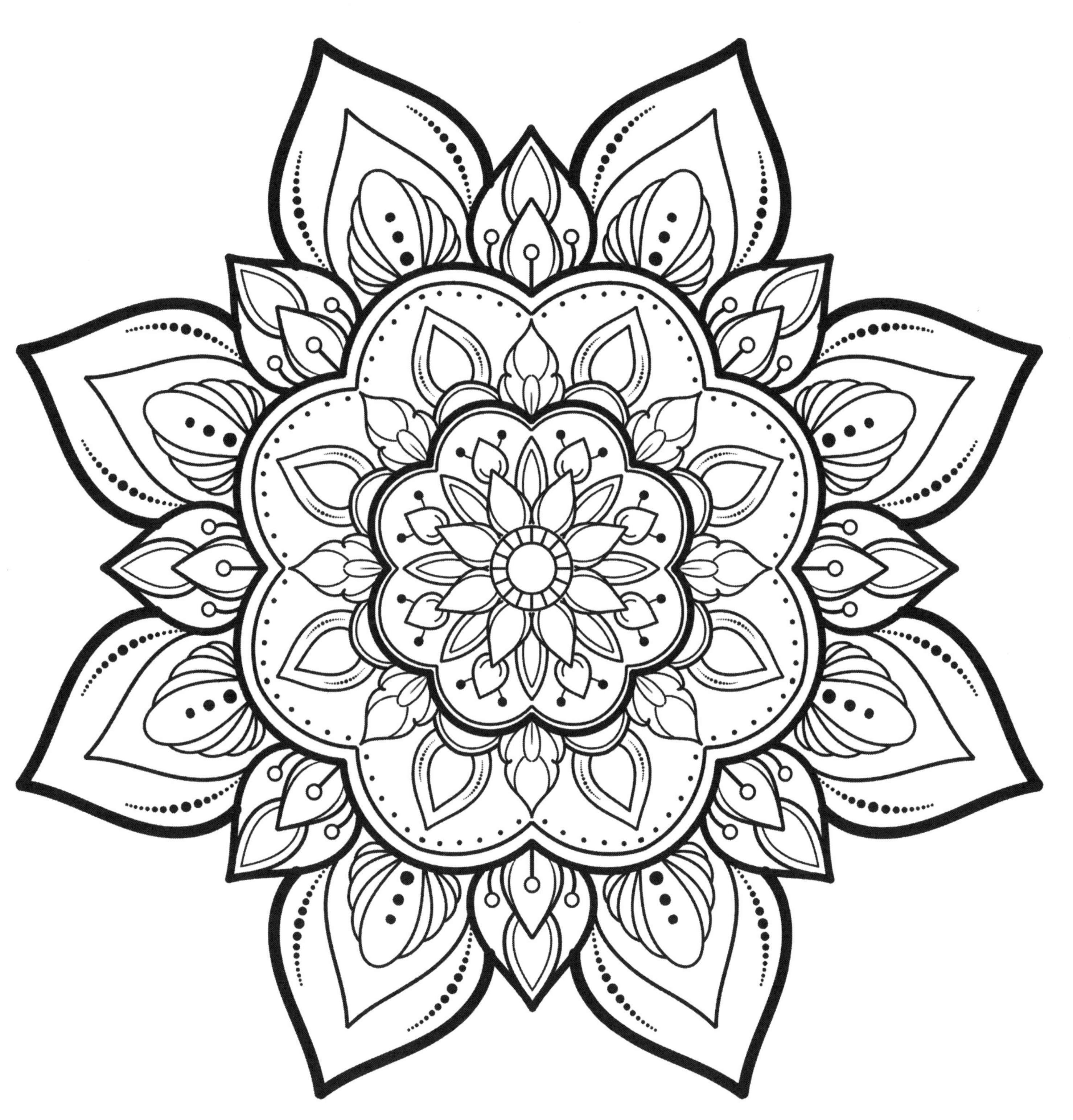

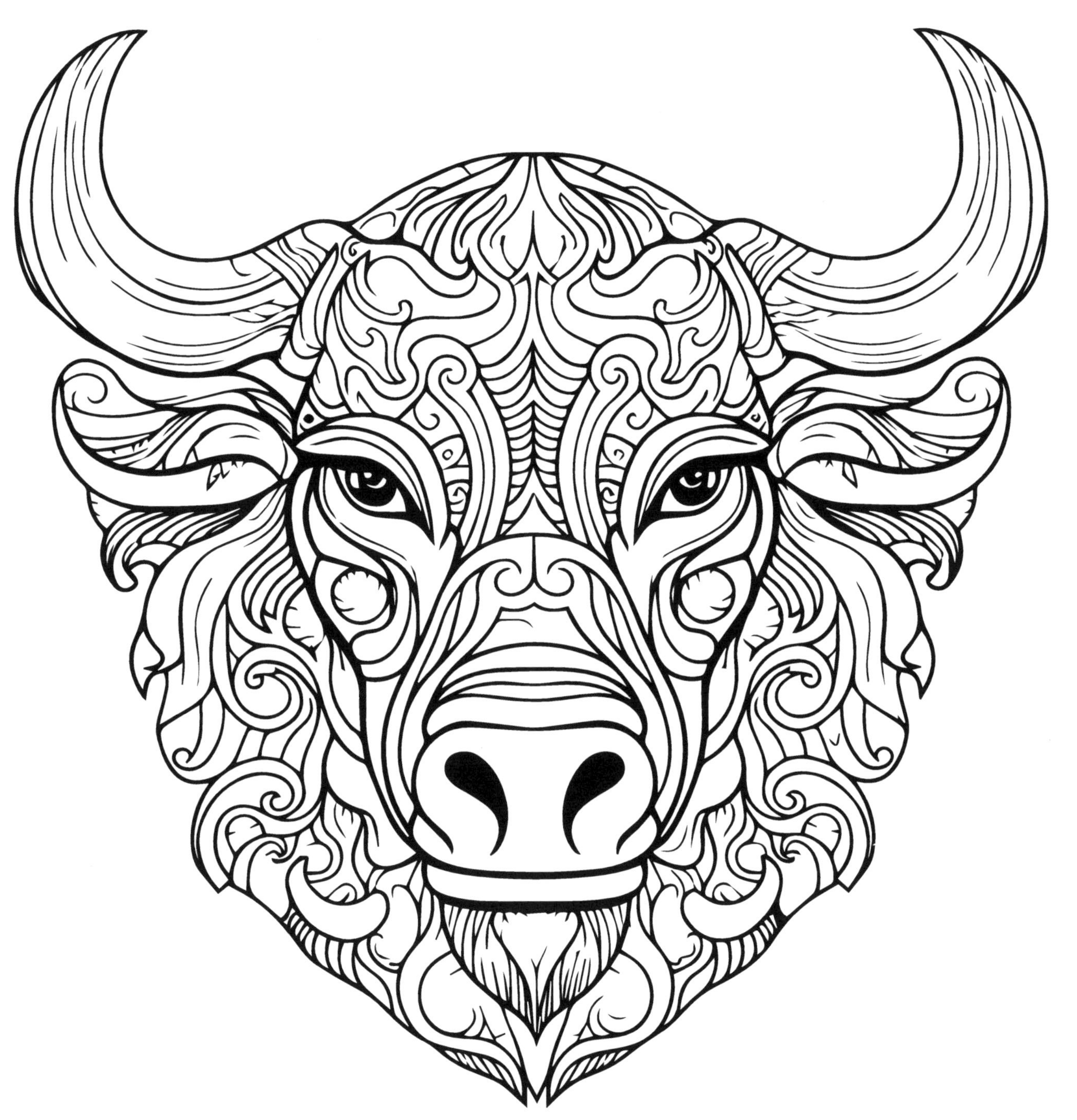

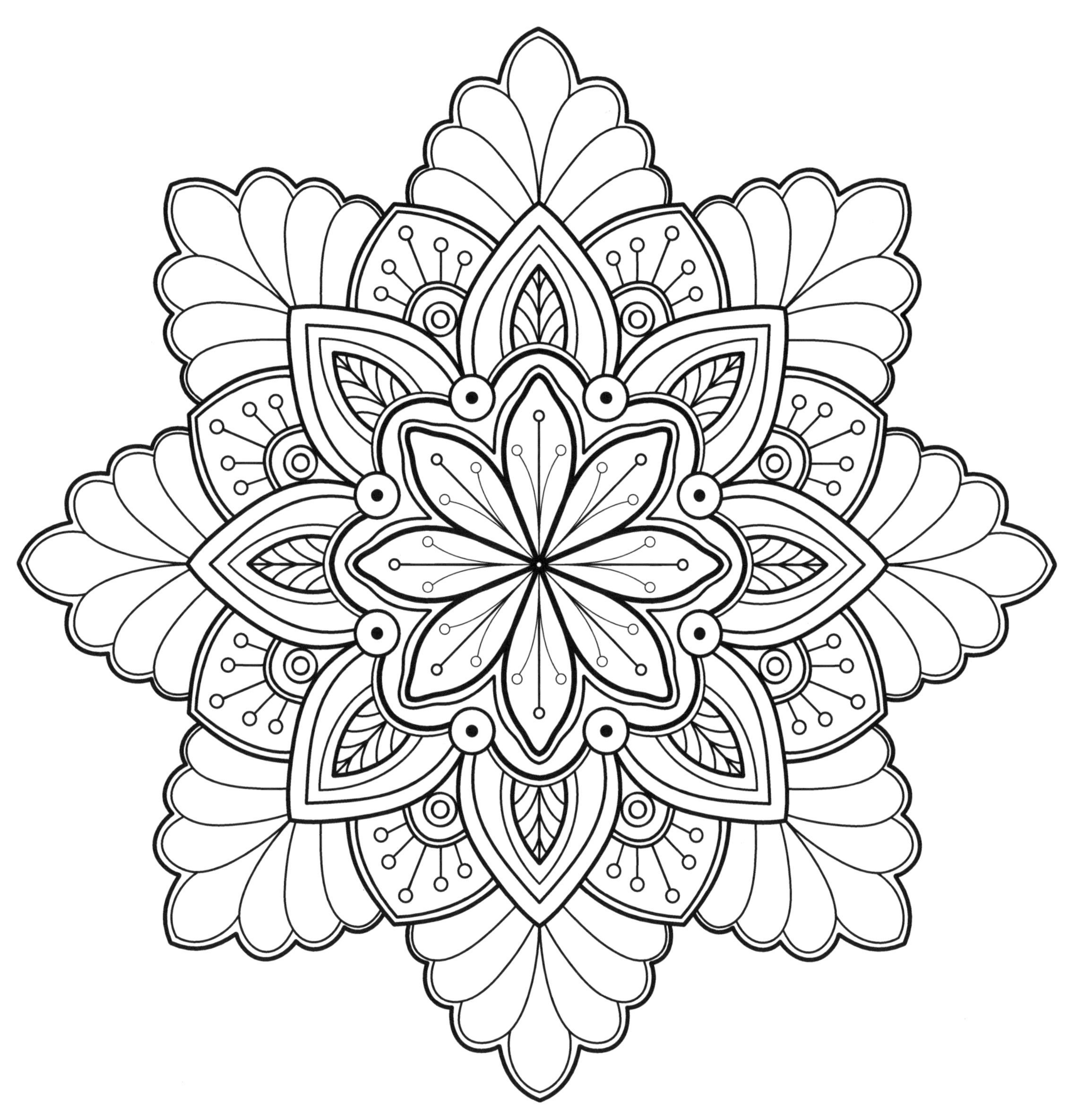

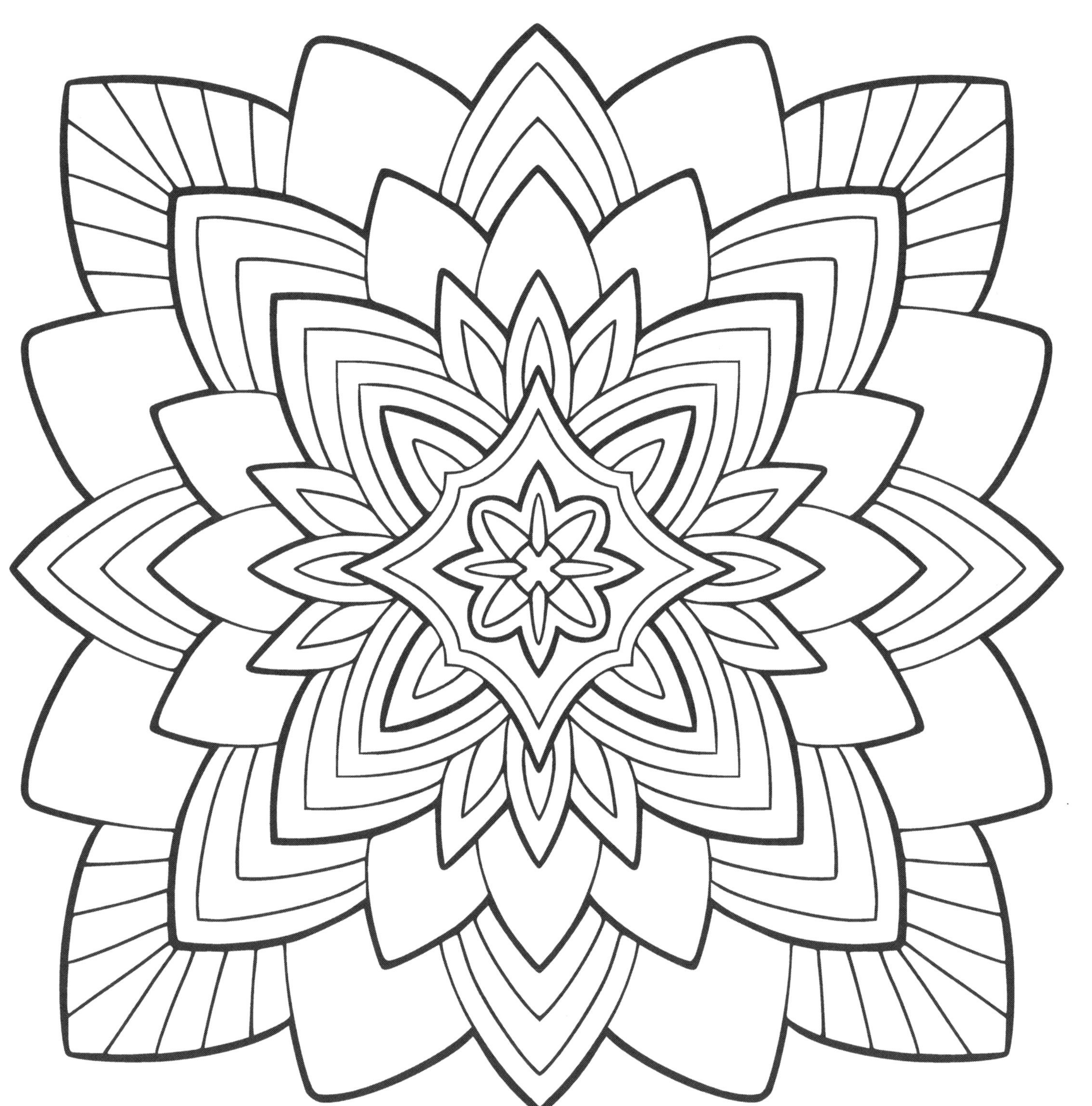

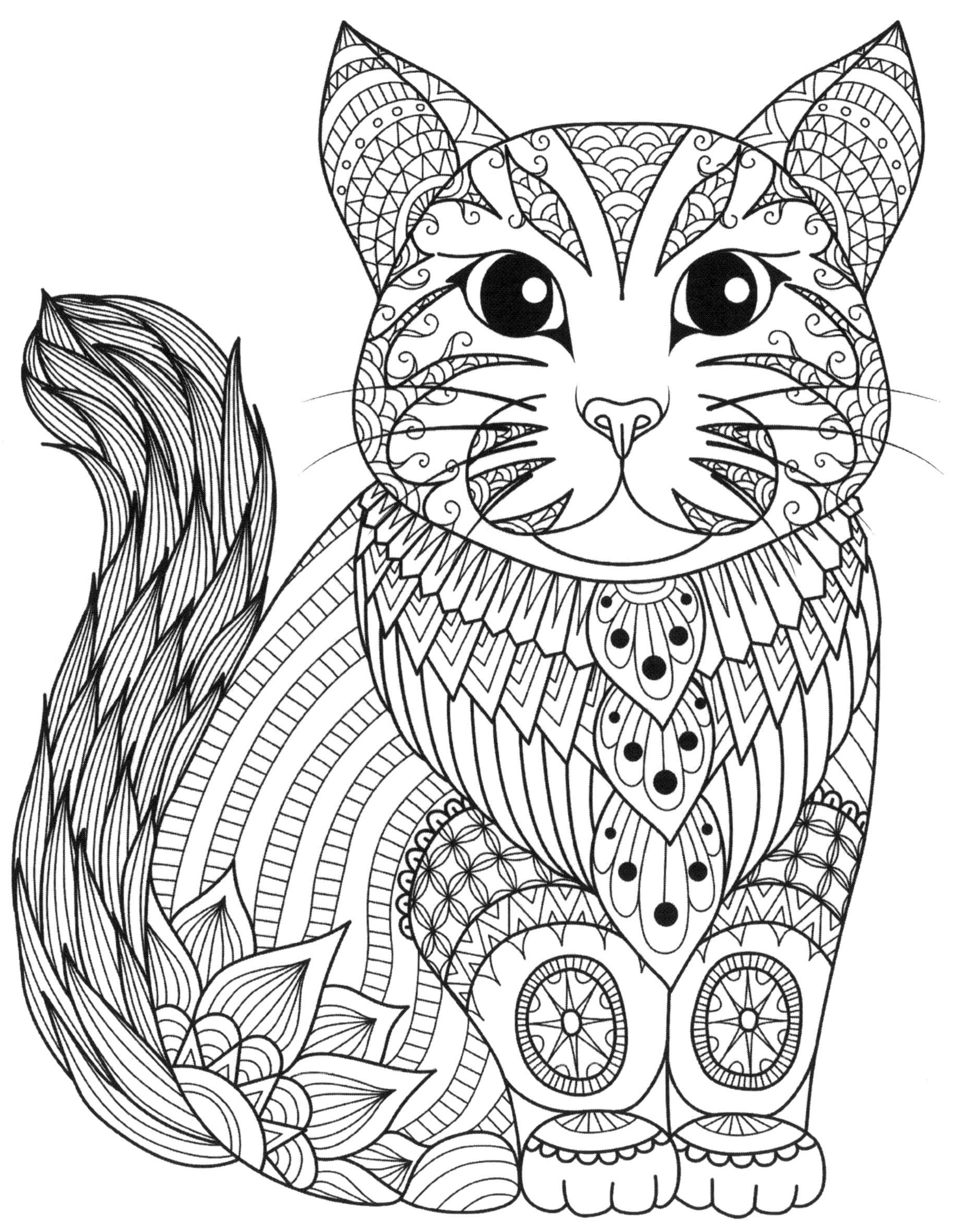

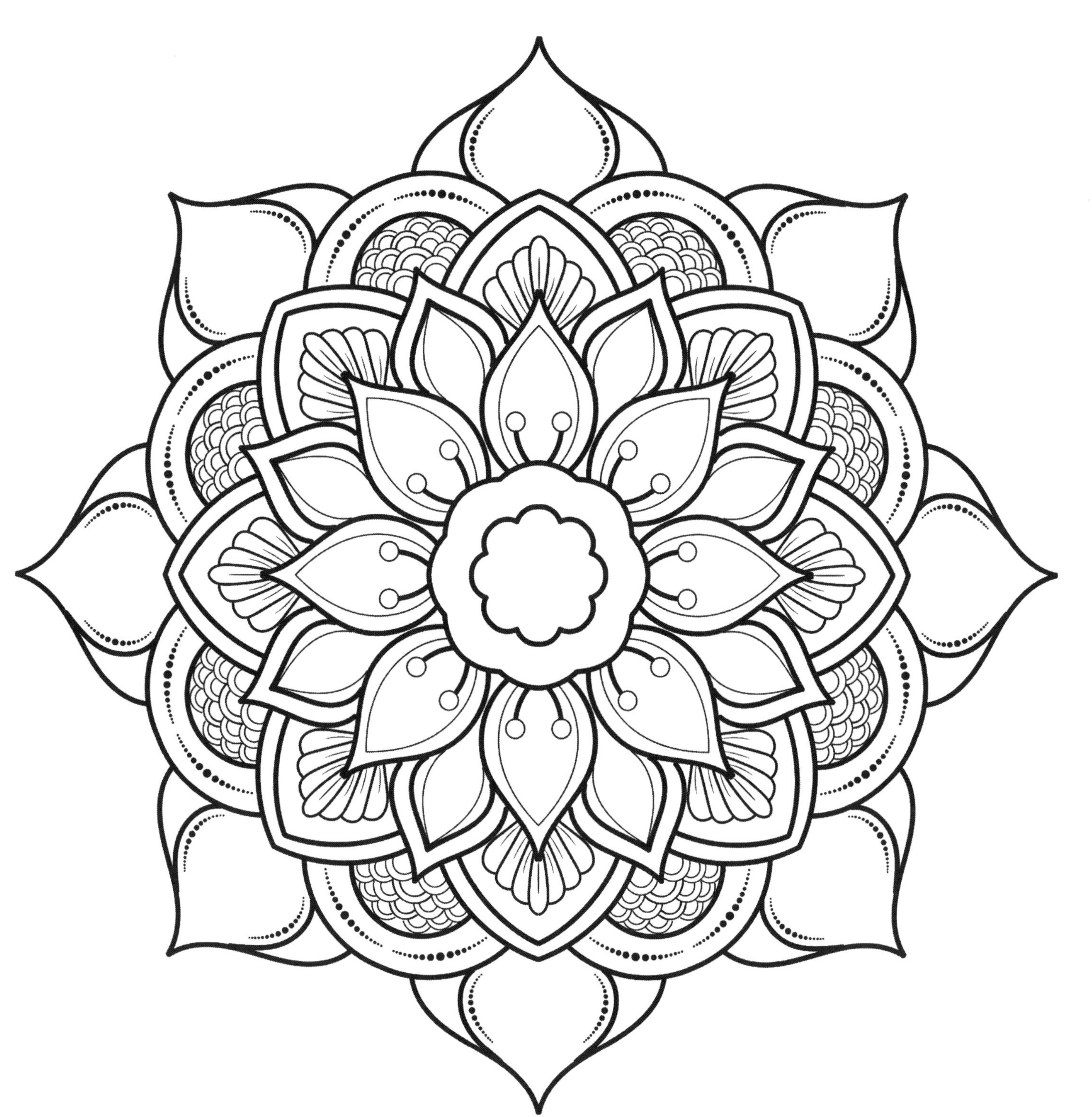

Made in the USA
Columbia, SC
07 June 2025